The Decroux Sourcebook

D1448627

The Decroux Sourcebook is the first point of reference for any student of the 'hidden master' of twentieth-century theatre.

This book collates a wealth of key material on Etienne Decroux, including:

- An English translation of Patrick Pezin's 'Imaginary Interview', in which Decroux discusses mime's place in the theatre.
- Previously unpublished articles by Decroux from France's Bibliothèque Nationale.
- Essays from Decroux's fellow innovators Eugenio Barba and Edward Gordon Craig, explaining the synthesis of theory and practice in his work.

Etienne Decroux's pioneering work in physical theatre is here richly illustrated not only by a library of source material, but also with a gallery of images following his life, work and influences.

The Decroux Sourcebook is an ideal companion to Thomas Leabhart's *Etienne Decroux* in the Routledge Performance Practitioners series, offering key primary and secondary resources to those conducting research at all levels.

Thomas Leabhart is an actor, director, writer and teacher who worked and studied with Etienne Decroux and performed under his direction. He is editor of the *Mime Journal*, and has published numerous articles on mime and theatre, as well as two books: *Modern and Post-Modern Mime* (Macmillan, 1989) and *Etienne Decroux* (Routledge, 2007).

Franc Chamberlain teaches Drama and Theatre Studies at University College Cork, Ireland, and is Visiting Professor in Performance Studies and Creative Practice at the University of Northampton, UK. He is the author of *Michael Chekhov* (Routledge, 2004) and co-editor of *Jacques Lecoq and the British Theatre* (Routledge, 2001).

The Decroux Sourcebook

- Edited by Thomas Leabhart and Franc Chamberlain

Routledge
Taylor & Francis Group

LONDON AND NEW YORK

First published 2008 by Routledge
2 Park Square, Milton Park, Abingdon,
Oxon OX14 4RN

Simultaneously published in the USA and
Canada
by Routledge
270 Madison Avenue, New York, NY
10016

*Routledge is an imprint of the Taylor &
Francis Group, an informa business*

Typeset in Sabon by Keystroke, 28 High
Street, Tettenhall, Wolverhampton

Printed and bound in Great Britain by
CPI Antony Rowe, Chippenham,
Wiltshire

*British Library Cataloguing in
Publication Data*
A catalogue record for this book is
available from the British Library

*Library of Congress Cataloging in
Publication Data*
Decroux, Etienne, 1898–1991.
The Decroux sourcebook / edited
by Thomas Leabhart and Franc
Chamberlain.
    p. cm.
    Consists chiefly of works by Decroux.
    Includes bibliographical references
and index.
    ISBN 978–0–415–40812–7
(hbk. : alk. paper) 1. Decroux, Etienne,
1898–1991. 2. Mime. I. Leabhart,
Thomas. II. Chamberlain, Franc.
III. Title.
PN1986.D43A25 2008
792.302′8092—dc22
[B]
2008018367

ISBN Pb: 978–0–415–47800–7

To Maximilien Decroux, and to the memory of Etienne and Suzanne Decroux.

To Lucy, Julian and Sophie: words are not enough.

Contents

CONTENTS

Illustrations

Acknowledgements

We would both like to thank Talia Rodgers, Minh-Ha Duong and Ben Piggott at Routledge for their support throughout this project and its changes, as well as Patrick Pezin of *Les Voies de l'acteur*. Sally Leabhart has provided immense and invaluable assistance through her translations from the French. We are also grateful to Librairie Théâtrale for permission to reproduce extracts from Etienne Decroux's *Paroles sur le mime*, and to Edward Gordon Craig's Estate, for permission to publish a translation of Craig's 'Enfin un créateur au théâtre' in *Arts*, 3 August 1945.

Thanks to Eugenio Barba for allowing us to reprint his essay 'The Hidden Master', which first appeared in *Mime Journal*. Most importantly we thank Maximilien Decroux for permission to include his father's previously published and unpublished texts. Unpublished texts come from the Fonds Etienne Decroux of the Bibliothèque Nationale in Paris. We would also like to add our sincere thanks to Young Tseng Wong for compiling the index.

In addition, Thomas Leabhart would like to thank his colleagues and students at Pomona College, and his colleagues throughout the world who specialize in teaching Etienne Decroux's Corporeal Mime.

Franc Chamberlain would like to thank colleagues and students at both University College Cork and Northampton University, especially Bernadette Sweeney, Bernadette Cronin, Jane Bacon and Vida Midgelow. The Division of Performance Studies at Northampton funded a term's study leave during the early stages of this project.

Part one

Introduction

Editors' introduction

This book documents the non-verbal, codified theatre tradition of Corporeal Mime passed from teacher to student in a way almost unknown in the West, but common in many Asian countries. Whereas the West's classical dance has a history of nearly four centuries, Corporeal Mime was created in the twentieth century. Etienne Decroux (1898–1991), the founder and creator of this living tradition, taught for six decades. Many of his students still practise and teach his work which subverts the prevailing paradigm: text-based theatre.[1]

Decroux himself (although a brilliant speaker and lapidary prose craftsman) encouraged among his students a healthy scepticism towards speaking or writing about things one could not do. He believed that until the word was made flesh, it was only so much hot air. He disdained intellectuals and others who were 'sitting down', in contrast to the Corporeal Mime who preferred to stand. He might have cautioned us against putting things into words lest people believe that the words alone could lead to understanding. And he would have defended his discoveries against people writing about them who had no practical knowledge of his intentions.

Yet despite the militantly non-verbal aspects of Decroux's work, these words by and about him form an essential part of his legacy. 'The Imaginary Interview', compiled by Patrick Pezin (pp. 61–160), organizes a collage of tape-recorded interviews and lectures, given by Decroux over a twenty-year period, around major themes: mime and dance, mime and puppets, mime and mask, etc. This material, made available here in English, was published in French in 2003 in a collection edited by Pezin. We also include previously unpublished articles by Decroux, archived in the Bibliothèque Nationale in Paris. These articles reveal more of Decroux's wit, his unfailing conviction and his intellectual rigour.

In addition to these new words by Decroux, we include two important essays about him, one by Edward Gordon Craig, the other by Eugenio Barba. Craig and Barba both knew Decroux (thirty years apart), and although not his students, they were deeply impressed by his new/old approach to theatre. When others who had not worked with him tried to write about Decroux, they often got it wrong. Never having done the physical work, they could not grasp his metaphysical, political or moral stance. Reducing him to yet one more twentieth-century intellectual ignores his monumental contribution as a theatre practitioner and innovator of a new theatrical vocabulary. Both Craig and Barba, themselves considerable innovators, intuited that Decroux's mostly non-verbal work was not primarily theoretical but instead an inseparable blend of theory *and* practice. Decroux's world view, strangely inaccessible to scholars who have never put their bodies into his shapes, requires a kind of kinaesthetic literacy which often runs counter to and even contradicts scholarly literacy, at least as we know it in most Western universities. Craig and Barba, however, made the intuitive leap.

History and future of Corporeal Mime

Etienne Decroux, born of working-class parents, became interested in politics, and, at age twenty-five, took a year off from his work as a manual labourer to study voice and diction as a way of furthering his political aspirations. He happened upon a class at Jacques Copeau's Ecole du Vieux-Colombier, where he quickly became enamoured with body work taught there: masked improvisation, Noh theatre, ballet, acrobatics and so on. His new political party became the theatre, more precisely his own developing vision of an artistic (artificial and articulated) theatre with a newly conceived actor at its centre; Decroux took Copeau's purism (bare stage) a step further (a nearly nude actor on a bare stage) and Corporeal Mime developed in that rarefied environment. Decroux reimagined the human body in an abstracted and systematic way without precedent, starting with what ballet had devised for legs and feet, and adding on rich possibilities obtained by articulating, in three dimensions, the trunk. As twentieth-century scientists sought the smallest particles of matter – cells and atoms – Decroux found the smallest articulations of the human keyboard. While the aesthetics might owe something to the ancient Noh, the mechanics were cubistically cutting edge.

While most people associate mime and pantomime (terms used sometimes today interchangeably, and throughout history variably) with silent storytelling, much of what one called mime or pantomime in the ancient world and for hundreds of years afterwards was seldom silent; often a chorus accompanied, or the mime performer himself spoke or sang. During brief periods (usually due to governmental restriction, as during the time of Louis XIV, or in nineteenth-century France) mime was exclusively silent; yet these gave rise to the misconception, still commonly held, that mime is silent storytelling. Decroux reacted strongly to these notions as he created a new form, Corporeal Mime, which de-emphasized face and hands and focused on the actor's trunk. His new mime marked a break from nineteenth-century pantomime, in whose silenced theatres the exercise became: what can I say without words? Decroux, who detested this kind of guessing game, often said, 'If you have something to say, why not just come out and say it?' He never imagined his ideal theatre should remain silent forever, but simply until the actor took control from directors, playwrights and other 'colonizers' of the theatre (Decroux 1985, 23–7).

Figure 1 The French pantomime Séverin (1863–1930) represents the kind of silent performance Decroux saw as a child, and about which he wrote:

> About the same time [1909, when Decroux was eleven], I saw a Pierrot who told his audience, without words, the tale of his love, his misfortune, his crime and his punishment.
>   The speaking actor is less garrulous.
>   This displeased me. (Decroux 1985, 14)

A contemporary article describes Séverin's performance, as Pierrot, in a four-act pantomime entitled 'Conscience': 'Throughout the entire performance not a word is spoken, music alone being relied upon to help reveal the pantomimist's emotions' (*New York Times*, 22 December 1908).

Decroux reversed this paradigm. He exchanged the completely covered body for an almost nude one; the emphasis on expressive face and hands replaced by inexpressive face and hands which neither promised nor threatened; the emphasis on plot for an almost plot-less performance, where causality could replace story line; and dim footlights exchanged for bright light from above.

If mime performers may speak, one might ask, how do they differ from ordinary actors? Again, painting with a broad brush, mimes have historically created their own verbal and non-verbal texts, and not been subject to directors or play-wrights. Decroux often said that plays should be performed first and written later, giving most power to actors, shifting it from a sedentary individual (the playwright) and giving it instead to an active group (the actors).

When thinking about the history of Corporeal Mime, we are considering something less than a century old, as Decroux laid most of the groundwork in the 1930s and continued developing it through the 1980s. With hindsight, Corporeal Mime may turn out to be (on one end of the spectrum) a fig-ment of that one man's maniacal imagination, or (on the other end) the beginning of a new theatre form – or something in between. Only time will tell if Decroux fills the role of a twentieth-century Zeami, as Kathryn Wylie-Marques suggests:

> Like Zeami, Decroux was intent on creating a mime based on elegance, inner beauty, and truth; for him, this meant fidelity to the laws of kinetic geometry applied to the moving body.
>
> (Wylie-Marques 1998, 115)

Decroux, obsessed with Corporeal Mime's uncertain future, often wondered aloud in his now-legendary Friday evening lectures if it would survive in the way he hoped. He knew that anything 'new' ran the risk of becoming assimilated by the prevailing paradigms. Perhaps that's why he went to such pains to distinguish Corporeal Mime from nineteenth-century pantomime, from dance, from speaking theatre and from cinema.

Inspired by his studies with Copeau, Suzanne Bing and others at the Vieux-Colombier, and by a collaboration with Jean-Louis Barrault, Decroux reimagined the human body in a musically analytical way, breaking it down into a keyboard that could, he hoped, play any melody the actor imagined. Through a distaste for silent pantomime, he developed a project much more aligned with that of his contemporary, Artaud, who wrote that:

> the theatre
> as I conceive it,

[is] a theatre of blood,
a theatre which, with each performance will have done
something
bodily
to the one who performs as well as to the one who comes
    to see others perform, but actually
the actors are not performing,
they are *doing*. [second emphasis added] (Artaud 1988,
    585)

In her kitchen, Madame Decroux once said something remarkably similar: 'The Corporeal Mime does not *pretend*, he *does*.' (The word in French for 'pretend' is *faire semblant*, which makes the citation more pungent: 'Le mime ne fait pas semblant, il fait.') Decroux's project recognized that creating illusions limited both actor and audience in a trite world of predictable vignettes. Like Grotowski, Decroux wanted to touch the audience deeply rather than simply entertain them. This reminds one of Grotowski's description (in a lecture at Eugenio Barba's International School of Theatre Anthropology in Copenhagen in 1995) of the principle of induction, whereby an electrical wire, attached to an energy source, runs parallel to another unattached wire in which one can detect a lesser energy; in the same way a receptive (Grotowski's word was 'unblocked') audience can absorb a measure of energy from actors who are charged through their technique and rehearsal process. (The relevant *Oxford English Dictionary*'s definition of induction: 'The action of inducting or bringing about an electric or magnetic state in a body by the proximity [without actual contact] of an electrified or magnetized body.')

So the emphasis shifts from 'what' (what is the performer doing?) to 'how' (is the performer, in Artaud's words, doing something bodily which changes – electrifies or magnetizes – himself and those who witness it?). Artaud would have called nineteenth-century white-faced pantomime 'corrupted' pantomime as the gestures represent words. He preferred 'pantomime which has not been corrupted':

By 'pantomime which has not been corrupted' I mean direct Pantomime in which the gestures – instead of representing words or sentences as in our European pantomime, which is only fifty years old and which is merely a distortion of the silent parts of Italian commedia – represent ideas, mental attitudes, aspects of natural objects or details. . . . [. . .]

This language, which evokes in the mind images of an intense natural (or spiritual) poetry, gives an idea of what it might mean for the theatre to have a poetry of space independent of spoken language.

(Artaud 1988, 233)

Decroux would call Artaud's 'poetry of space' Corporeal Mime, which bore more resemblance to cubism, surrealism, collage and abstract expressionism than to charmingly decorative nineteenth-century pantomime.

Decroux's project prefigures by decades the phenomenon described by Hans-Thies Lehmann as postdramatic theatre:

The physical body, whose gestic vocabulary in the eighteenth century could still be read and interpreted virtually like a text, in postdramatic theatre has become its own reality which does not 'tell' this or that emotion but through its presence *manifests* itself as the site of inscription of collective history.

(Lehmann 2006, 97)

We ought not to be surprised that Artaud's writings contain implicit or even explicit references to Decroux, as they knew each other well enough and Decroux spoke of their relationship (see 'The Imaginary Interview', pp. 95–6). In addition they each mentored Jean-Louis Barrault, and all three had different degrees of connection with the work of Jacques Copeau who had sought a Commedia 'using contemporary types and subjects' (Rudlin and Paul 1990, 153). Though one may argue convincingly that the seeds of Corporeal Mime come directly from Copeau's Ecole du Vieux-Colombier, one may also find several other lesser influences, not least of all

Decroux's working-class background as a manual labourer and a militant socialist.

Copeau's (and subsequently Decroux's) interest in the Commedia dell'arte was shared with others searching for a new theatre such as the Russians, Stanislavsky, Meyerhold and Vakhtangov, but also the peripatetic and hugely influential Englishman Edward Gordon Craig, whom Copeau visited in Italy at the start of World War I, and whom Decroux recognizes in *Words on Mime* as a primary inspiration for Corporeal Mime.

In 'The First Dialogue' (1905), Craig's Stage Director claims: 'The Art of the Theatre has sprung from action – movement – dance' (Craig 2009, 73). While Craig looked to the past or to other cultures for theatres he admired, in tune with the spirit of the times, he wasn't interested in re-creating what was lost, but in finding new forms. As Isadora Duncan wrote of the connection of her work to ancient Greek dance: 'I do not mean to say *copy* it, *imitate* it; but to *breathe its life, to recreate it in one's self with personal inspiration*' (Preston 2005, 275). Likewise, Copeau's innovative bare stage owes an enormous debt to what he called the Golden Ages of theatre, which had similar bare stages: the ancient Greeks, the Noh, the Commedia dell'arte and the Elizabethan theatre, as well as the modern circus ring. And Decroux's Corporeal Mime body, with all its modernist and purist aspects, often resembles the ancient statuary we can see in museums like the Getty Villa in Malibu, representing veiled dancers and mimes of antiquity.

We should include the dance of Laban, Wigman, Shawn and St Denis, Graham, Humphrey and Isadora Duncan with this list of those looking to develop a new art of movement, but these were all easily assimilated under the dance umbrella and, although Corporeal Mime might take temporary shelter there, as it differed in its basic DNA (a dramatic rather than lyric art) it never really belonged there. Decroux considered that Corporeal Mime's rooted, Promethean lower centre of gravity and imitation of work movements clearly distinguished it from dance. (True, Laban, Graham and others advocated a lower centre of gravity, but Decroux did so explicitly because work movements – counterweights – required it. These work movements give Corporeal Mime a preponderance of 'bound flow' and gravitas, more common in drama and less so in dance, which even in its heaviest manifestations is more airborne than Corporeal Mime.) Nor did it belong with spoken theatre, which seems almost permanently wedded to the playwright. While Artaud might have wanted the theatre to be free from the playwright in order to speak its own language, its own 'poetry of space', he is in some ways less of a kindred spirit to Decroux than Craig is. Artaud has remained, since his death, central to the study of theatre, his writings inspiring the avant-garde of 1960s' Europe and of America and continuing to inform both theoretical writings and performance practice.

Artaud, for all the immense influence of his ideas of the theatre as plague, never developed practices that have been passed down, while Decroux carved out Corporeal Mime, inspiring through teaching rather than polemic, a living practice passed on through the bodies of his students. And if we are to take the transmission of practices as key to the discussion, we would have to concede that Craig also failed to do that. If we are looking for a set of corporeal teachings that have been passed down, perhaps we should look to Meyerhold's biomechanics: they have attained a huge reputation since his death, but, until quite recently, with very few people who had actually studied the practice. We might argue that Meyerhold's reputation was primarily based on his directorial profile as theatre studies indeed shifted away from the playwright, but only towards the director rather than the performer.

Craig, Artaud, Copeau, Stanislavsky and Meyerhold held their places in the academy as representatives of the rise of the director. Meyerhold's biomechanics were far more likely to have been familiar through photographs in books such as Braun's *Meyerhold on Theatre* than through any engagement in actor-training or spectating. There were attempts, by the Living Theatre, for example, to use biomechanics, but they effectively galvanized photographs and descriptions from an article by Mel Gordon (1974), and galvanism only ever gave the illusion of life. In an article ten years later, Gordon wrote that he watched the Living Theatre's demonstration with 'something between horror and amusement' for 'while the poses the actors had copied from the photographs in my article were correct, all the transitions and body rhythms were wrong' (Gordon 1984, 13).

There are reasons for the Living Theatre's problems, as Jonathan Pitches makes clear: 'Stalin's eradication of biomechanics was so chillingly successful because it silenced the practitioners, those who were able to pass on the physical record of the work' (Pitches 2006, 66). Nonetheless, footage of Meyerhold's work has become available in recent years, and two teachers, with very differing styles, Gennady Bogdanov and Alexei Levinsky, have begun teaching regularly outside Russia. But the range of material that has survived is very limited, being reduced, as Pitches indicates, to 'five essential biomechanical etudes' (2006, 65), which is an astonishingly small amount of material when compared with the quantity of Decroux's work that survives.

How are we to explain the high profile, in the academy, of Meyerhold's biomechanics, compared to Decroux's Corporeal Mime? Is it simply that Meyerhold was more visible as a director and theoretician? Or might it be that Meyerhold, despite his comment that words should be the 'froth on a sea of movement', is more easily assimilated to a history of theatre that still manages to keep the written text as central, even when it shifts from an emphasis on the playwright to an emphasis on the director? Meyerhold can be seen as attempting to create a movement vocabulary that would complement, or serve, the written text, whereas both Decroux and Lecoq wanted to supplant (or at least greatly reduce the importance of) speech, written beforehand or otherwise.

Decroux was neither famous as a director (he directed only two traditional plays in his life), nor as a theoretician (most people find *Words on Mime* impenetrable), but better known as a teacher for over fifty years. He attracted occasional attention as the teacher of Marcel Marceau and Jean-Louis Barrault, but was steadfastly ignored in the academy. It is important to distinguish Decroux's work from that of his countryman Jacques Lecoq, but there are similarities in that they were regarded as working in a marginal area of theatre or dance. Lecoq, for example, after forty years of teaching an international clientele, was simply identified in the dance section of the French entry to the *World Encyclopaedia of Contemporary Theatre* as a 'mime' who 'later discovered masks' (Nagy and Rouyer 1994, 309; Chamberlain and Yarrow 2002, 4–5).

The Ecole Jacques Lecoq in Paris included mime in its title until the early 1990s, but Lecoq's view of mime was closer to Decroux's than was the popular conception of mime as silent storytelling. In 1987, Lecoq parodied the mime who 'pulled a face' or gesticulated 'crying for help' and described such mimes as suffering from a 'theatrical malady' (Lecoq 1987, cited in Murray and Keefe 2007, 19). Murray and Keefe suggest that it is this view of mime as a 'theatrical malady' that has held sway in the academy and this might offer another possibility for why Decroux's work has received little critical attention, even though it had nothing whatever to do with pulling faces or gesticulating, and was in fact a strong reaction against that clichéd work.

Starting from the same artistic parent, Jacques Copeau, and uncle, Gordon Craig, Decroux and Lecoq, each in quite different ways, challenged the playwright's centrality, as did Artaud, who also belongs in the tradition of Copeau, having studied with Charles Dullin. Copeau, who wanted to strengthen the actor's performance skills through study of ballet, acrobatics, improvisation, mask building and masked acting, never intended to jettison the text in performance; but the rediscovery of the creativity of the actor was always going to tend in this direction and became manifest in the case of Lecoq and Decroux.

Kathryn Wylie-Marques's observation that Decroux continued the shamanic line in mime, while Lecoq continued a carnivalesque one, seems apt. In addition to this huge difference in their professional work, they also seemed quite different in temperament, disposition, dress and demeanour: Decroux always more of an 'outsider' – long grey hair, uncon-ventional clothing – while Lecoq could have been mistaken for a banker, in his neat suit and short, carefully coiffed hair, or in his work clothes (dark athletic trousers and matching zipper-closed, long-sleeved top) like the gym teacher he had once been.

For his last decades, Decroux taught in the basement of his very modest house (a small cottage, really) while, at the same time, Lecoq had, by comparison, quite a grand school, much larger than Decroux's tiny basement, and with the secretaries and other administrative support Decroux conspicuously lacked. Lecoq, following in the line of Copeau, employed many other teachers to help, whereas Decroux trusted only his senior students and sometimes his son to teach a few of the classes, while he himself taught most of them. Those who attended Decroux's school knew of the remarkable price difference in Lecoq's and Decroux's tuition (perhaps a factor of each school's distinctly different structure). Decroux proudly (almost defiantly) had the lowest prices in Paris (which enabled him to summarily expel any student who lacked complete commitment, as he didn't need their tuition), and Decroux's students imagined, correctly or incorrectly, that only people with fellowships or government grants could pay Lecoq's fee. Self-taught and working-class to the core, Decroux knew he presided over a kind of cottage industry, and often spoke proudly of the 'style maison'. He extolled the artisan who worked with his hands, one who had a direct connection with his work and his customers, a person who was already quickly disappearing from the Parisian landscape in the last years of Decroux's teaching.

Regardless of their different styles, however, both Decroux and Lecoq adumbrated postdramatic theatre, where the body becomes more important than text:

> The body becomes the centre of attention, not as a carrier of meaning but in its physicality and gesticulation. The central theatrical sign, the actor's body, refuses to serve signification. Postdramatic theatre often presents itself as an auto-sufficient physicality, which is exhibited in its intensity, gestic potential, auratic 'presence' and internally, as well as externally, transmitted tensions.
>
> (Lehmann 2006, 95)

Both Decroux and Lecoq succeeded in upsetting the ancient hierarchy in which the actor's job was to speak and illustrate the author's text. Now, '[t]he body becomes the only subject matter' (Lehmann 2006, 96). Of course, Decroux and Lecoq were not lone harbingers, but they were among the most militant in their struggle.

If the nineteenth century was the century of the playwright, and the twentieth century the century of the director, might the twenty-first century become the century of the actor, working on the foundations established by Copeau, Craig, Artaud and Meyerhold, and especially, we might argue, Etienne Decroux?

1931: A year of convergence

> Around the same years that the lucid and painful curses of Antonin Artaud began to resonate, an event occurred in the kingdom of the actor. Near 1931, mime was reborn in France under the name of 'corporeal mime.'
>
> (Lorelle 1974, 105)

According to Yves Lorelle, 1931 was an important year in the development of Corporeal Mime, the art which Etienne Decroux first glimpsed in 1923, when the twenty-five-year-old manual labourer – who had saved enough money to live for a year without working – enrolled in voice and speech classes at the Ecole du Vieux-Colombier. While studying voice, he took classes in masked improvisation which gave birth to Decroux's life-long research. Afterwards, he became a stage, film and radio actor while developing his true passion, Corporeal Mime.

> [Decroux's] first offensive against the text occurred in the Théâtre Lancry in 1931. He performed, with his wife, *La Vie Primitive*, 'corporeal' mimodrama which they developed together. A single performance was given.
>
> (Lorelle 1974, 107)

Decroux's 'offensive against the text' had as its goal the placement of the actor squarely at the centre of the dramatic endeavour, displacing the playwright and sending him into exile, evicting the other 'alien arts' – costuming, décor, music, dance – as well.

> The meeting between Jean-Louis Barrault and Etienne Decroux is the second act of the war of these expert marksmen of the theatre, these 'corporeal mimes.' It happened on the stage of Dullin's theatre, the future Atelier – during the year 1931.
>
> (Lorelle 1974, 108)

While acting with Charles Dullin's company, and teaching in his school, Decroux met Jean-Louis Barrault in 1931. Barrault helped Decroux in the early elaboration of Corporeal Mime (see Barrault 1972 and 1984). Decroux and Barrault both moved in circles frequented by Artaud, who briefly apprenticed with Dullin, mentored Barrault and directed Decroux in at least one production.

Nicola Savarese's article '1931: Antonin Artaud Sees Balinese Theatre at the Paris Colonial Exposition' (2001) gives us important details about the Balinese performances which influenced Artaud's nascent view of a new Western theatre. Savarese writes that:

> it is very clear that Artaud wanted to use Balinese theatre as both example and confirmation of something of which he had become convinced during that period: that the theatre must have its own language, a language that is not the same as the language of words but which is based on the actor's physicality.
>
> (Savarese 2001, 51)

I imagine another article, entitled '1931: Etienne Decroux Sees Cambodian Theatre at the Paris Colonial Exposition', which might argue that, for Decroux, the Cambodians provided a comparable example and confirmation as the Balinese had for Artaud. While we have little direct evidence of this (Decroux did not publish an article about the Cambodians, as Artaud had about the Balinese), what we do know is intriguing and suggestive.

Sasagawa Hideo writes that although the Royal Ballet of Cambodia did not attend the 1931 Paris Colonial Exposition, a substitute troupe, directed by Soy Sangvong, the wife of a member of the royal family, was sent instead to perform at the very popular and spectacular model of Angkor Wat, the sensation of the Exposition (Hideo 2005, 428). In 1935, a travel writer in Cambodia described her meeting with Sangvong:

> The leader of the Angkor troupe is Princess Wongat Soysangvane, a member of the old Cambodian nobility. Her headquarters, and that of her troupe (except in the tourist season) are at Phnom Penh, where all the elaborately embroidered and bejewelled costumes worn by the dancers are made by her own clever fingers. . . . The head-dresses are modelled in the art-studios of the Museum, and are all exact copies of those in the bas-reliefs. Madame speaks French fluently; and has many tales to tell of the Great Adventure of 1931, when she took her troupe to Paris to perform at the Colonial Exhibition at Vincennes.
>
> (Ponder 1936, 240)

Based on the following facts, one might argue that this is the troupe Decroux probably saw.

During the years 1968–72, Etienne Decroux in the basement studio of his home in a suburb of Paris frequently mentioned the present-yet-absent faces of the statues from Angkor in Cambodia as the ideal expression for Corporeal Mime. In 1968, Decroux was a seventy-year-old master teacher in his prime, still physically vital, and one who had boiled his teaching down to the essential. From the intensity of his descriptions, one could tell that these Angkor faces were part of what he treasured deeply, a key element of his teaching. He didn't just mention them in passing; he ardently urged us to visit the Musée Guimet to see these statues first-hand

15

and to sense how much expression passed through those supposedly expressionless faces. In his life-long rebellion against the expressive face and hands of nineteenth-century pantomime, Decroux had found a strong and ancient ally, an Asian precursor to Copeau's noble mask.

One French journalist who witnessed the performances of Cambodian dancers in 1931 wrote:

> It is generally thought that Cambodian dances are nothing more than processions or confused tangles of harmonious plastic poses. It seems as if it is not possible to refer to Cambodian dancers without using the term 'hieratic.' . . . All the feelings have been foreseen and codified, as has been the way they are expressed. The face remains completely impassive beneath its white make-up but the body has means of expression that can reveal the movements of the very soul.
>
> (Florisoone in Savarese 2001, 72–3)

Ponder describes the white make-up in more detail:

> [I]t is difficult to recognize their vivacious expressive features in the creamy-white uniformity into which their curiously flat 'make-up' has transformed them. They might almost have been whitewashed, so thickly are their faces plastered over with an opaque paste which destroys all expression, and on which the lips and eyebrows . . . stand out in startling contrast.
>
> (Ponder 1936, 241)

The impassive face, the codified and highly articulate bodily movements and the 'plastic poses' as well as the use of the term 'hieratic' (formal, stylized and related to sacred persons or offices) all remind us of elements found in Decroux's own developing Corporeal Mime of 1931, the same year he wrote his first 'proper piece of writing on art' (Decroux 1985, 23–7) entitled 'Partial Incarnation of the Future Actor'.

Another reviewer describes the specific pieces the Cambodians performed in 1931:

Three dances: one to extend a greeting, the fight between a white monkey and a black one, and, to finish, the story of Prince Soryavong, an elegant subject worthy of our fables or those of Boccaccio.

The orchestra, composed of *kongs* in the shape of a horseshoe made of seventeen little gongs joined together, is made up of, among other instruments, twin drums, flutes, cymbals and of a curious instrument made up of wooden strips. The dancers, dressed in sumptuous costumes, wearing golden or silver-plate tiaras, depending on their rank, adorned sometimes by grimacing masks, dripping with gold jewellery encrusted with precious stones, expressed with unchanging gestures all human feelings. Each action, each nuance of gesture, handed down from generation to generation. And this art, which is neither lascivious nor vulgar and by which the legs arced, the arms vibrate like reptiles, hands curved upward, the head and back drawn upward, attained a nobility and a religious emotion which made us pass from humble reality to the world of legend.

(Cadilhac 1931, 564)

Those of us who know Decroux's work well and first-hand, recognize in the phrase 'a nobility and a religious emotion which made us pass from humble reality to the world of legend' an exact description of Decroux's passionate convictions about Corporeal Mime.

In addition to Etienne Decroux's frequent references to the facial expression of certain Cambodian statues (which seem to mirror the facial expressions in the Cambodian dances Decroux probably saw), he also devised a quarter turn which he called 'The Cambodian'. This cubistically articulated movement begins in the foot and leg, which first 'wake up' before they pull the body into a turn. Additionally, Leonard Pitt recalls Decroux's appreciation of the articulations and isolations of Cambodian dance during Pitt's years of study, the mid-1960s (email to Leabhart, 21 February 2008). Steven Wasson, too, describes a movement of hands and fingers which Decroux called 'les doigts de la danseuse cambodgienne' in Decroux's classes in the 1980s, a half-century after he would have seen the performance which inspired it (email to Leabhart, 2 July 2007). In searching for more specific proof, Leabhart met with Decroux's son, Maximilien, on 9 July 2007 in Boulogne (in the small house which had once been his father's home and school). Leabhart asked Decroux-*fils* if he thought his father had seen the Cambodian dance at the Colonial Exposition of 1931. He replied that he knew his father had attended the Exposition, and that he knew he had seen Cambodian dance, although he could not verify that the performance in question was the one at the Colonial Exposition. He jokingly said that one could assert that his father had seen it at the Exposition if one wanted to, and that no one could contradict him.

One more tantalizing detail: Decroux's great friend Paul Bellugue, with whom he performed lecture demonstrations, and whose knowledge of classical sculpture and anatomy Decroux found essential in the formulation of Corporeal Mime, spent five years, from 1925 to 1930, in Cambodia and wrote articles about Cambodian art (Bellugue 1963, 285).

Bellugue describes a moment from the Cambodian dance:

Thus, like the idols in the temples, like a god descended from the heavenly palaces of Indra, the queen, a thousand years ago, was carried off on the golden palanquin towards the dance room. Smiling and secretive, she floated along, gently rocking above the shoulders and the bowed heads, into the bluish sweltering heat of evening.

Thus, similarly dressed and for the same celebrations, the king's dancers move towards the Phnom Penh palace today.

(Bellugue 1963, 309)

And the photograph accompanying this page of Bellugue's text? The same one which appears in the 22 August 1931 issue of *L'Illustration*, detailing the Cambodians' performance at the Colonial Exposition (Cadilhac 1931, 565).

Finally, and perhaps most conclusively, the late Guy Benhaim's 1992 dissertation on Etienne Decroux confirms

Figure 2 Figures 2 and 3 are photographs from the 22 August 1931 issue of *L'Illustration* depicting Cambodian dancers, whom Decroux probably saw at the Colonial Exposition that year.

Figure 3 Cambodian dancers, 1931.

that, according to some of Decroux's last assistants (he does not give their names), Decroux saw the Cambodians in Paris in 1931 (Benhaim 1992, 106).

Whatever Decroux saw, and whenever he actually saw it, Cambodian dance left a lasting and thrilling impression on his imagination, as it had on another French genius, Auguste Rodin, who made drawings of the Cambodians when they visited Marseilles nine years earlier.

But Decroux's poorly documented encounter finally produced a concrete acting technique, unlike Artaud's well-documented one, which produced primarily theory. Whereas Savarese contends that Artaud's meeting with the Balinese confirmed his conviction that 'theatre must have its own language, a language that is not the same as the language of words but which is based on the actor's physicality', we argue that Decroux's encounter with the Cambodians also confirmed his similar conviction. However, and this is where the result was finally different, due to ill health, Artaud was unable to follow through with the actual creation of a Western equivalent to the Balinese dance-theatre 'language'. In addition to Artaud's poor health, Savarese suggests that his 'poetic nature . . . [his] mental indiscipline' kept him from practising a 'rigorous actor's art based on discipline' (2001, 73). Decroux, however, spent a half-century on his project, the creation of Corporeal Mime, a part of which he attributed to some early impressions of Cambodian dance-theatre.

Leonard Pronko in his groundbreaking study *Theatre East and West* describes another important aspect of Artaud's fascination with the Balinese, using words which could aptly describe Decroux's impressions of the Cambodians:

> Through the dancer, who has become a kind of medium at the same time he is an artist, we the audience are put into contact, however dimly, with some experience beyond that of our everyday physical world. We are somehow brought into touch with what Artaud would call an absolute.
>
> (Pronko 1967, 14)

During Leonard Pitt's years of study with Decroux in the 1960s, Pitt remembers Decroux explaining in class that the student-actor must 'empty yourself so that this place can be filled with the soul of God' (email to Leabhart, 21 February 2008). In an attempt to move the student into that absolute world which Decroux imagined as Corporeal Mime, a world quite different from that of the theatre and cinema acting of Decroux's day, he invited his young 'converts' to undertake a kind of shamanic voyage. Decroux's first disciple, Jean-Louis Barrault, writes in shamanic terms (or perhaps derived from his study of the Cabala with Artaud) that he:

> understood, during this night of initiation, that the whole problem of theatre is to make the Silence vibrate. Melt this Silence. Travel upstream. When the river flows into the sea, it dies; its estuary is the site of its illness . . . It's a question of going against the flow to return to the source, to the birth, to the essence.
>
> (Barrault 1972, 77)

Artaud's and Barrault's acceptance of Asian influence, which revitalized and confirmed their already firmly established differences from mainstream theatre practice of their time, may not be the first time East has revitalized West. Enrico Fulchignoni argues that in the early development of the Commedia dell'arte, 'the words gradually untwined themselves from the written text and improvisation took over' (1990, 30). Fulchignoni writes that

> relations with the Orient are intensified during the late Middle Ages. There are no longer just a few isolated pioneers but a real flow of information and systematic exploring, along with commercial interests and trade [. . .]. [A]s a result of contacts between the two worlds the scale and value of things can only develop in completely new directions.
>
> (Fulchignoni 1990, 34)

This description fits perfectly the Colonial period, when commerce and artistic cross-pollination went hand-in-hand,

and when, as in the early fifteenth century, 'displacements of people occurred, as well as of cultural property' (Fulchignoni 1990, 40).

> When one is dealing with the written or printed word, it is possible to prove these connections [between East and West]. But when one is concerned with something which cannot be defined in words – the ephemeral, the instantaneous, the magical, as in the case of theatre – one has to proceed on an act of faith. In a century of fervent expressive power, as prevailed in the period before the explosion of the Renaissance, the dialogue between East and West never stopped for a second. Each new proof of the existence of such interaction is further assertion of the fragility of Eurocentristic theories of cultural reality.
>
> (Fulchignoni 1990, 41)

Fulchignoni argues convincingly that Asian theatre forms likely had some effect on the beginnings of Commedia dell'arte. And I argue that the Balinese and Cambodian forms, respectively, that Artaud and Decroux witnessed, confirmed and inspired their own work towards a new actor-centred (rather than text-based) theatre. In Artaud's case, because of his temperament and poor health, his work was episodic, and resulted more in theory than in practice. In Decroux's case, his work became a life-long obsession with elaborating an aesthetic and a codified technique appropriate to a newly articulated actor, on a bare stage, at the centre of a theatre from which the playwright had been evicted.

Note

1   Miranda Welby-Everard's 'Imagining the Actor: The Theatre of Claude Cahun' (2006) documents how the Parisian avant-garde of the 1920s and 30s valued many of the same things Decroux did: artificiality, masks, puppets, 'pure art', 'transformation of the actor/dancer into a living effigy through reduction to a system of lines, shapes and colours', 'denial of characterization, set and plot, the abandonment of human narrative and the removal of the standard structure of exposition, development,

crisis and dénouement', the actor 'concealed within a body-mask and operated like a clockwork toy', 'eradicating the human face', etc. But whereas Decroux continued in this line for half a century, creating a highly articulated corporeal vocabulary in the service of this ideology, many of his contemporaries passed quickly through this phase, without it becoming the determining element of their work. One might say that many of his ideas were in the spirit of his time, and that he persevered.

At last a creator in the theatre, from the theatre

Edward Gordon Craig

[First published in *Arts*, 3 August 1945, translated from the French by Sally Leabhart.]

More than a thousand audience members packed the theatre of the Maison de la Chimie on 27 June to attend a performance by Etienne Decroux, Jean-Louis Barrault and Eliane Guyon in their 'Programme of Corporeal Mime'. There they heard my name pronounced several times by Mr Jean Dorcy when he explained to them the overriding idea of the event.

Mr Dorcy told his audience that this Decroux–Barrault performance had been inspired by some idea which had come from me. Now, I attended that remarkable performance, and watching it, I realized that it was an attempt, developed slowly over time, to create an art for the stage. But I didn't see how I could claim to have earned, by my actions or my words, Mr Dorcy's great compliment – although I would have been sincerely honoured to have done so. Mr Dorcy can perhaps indicate something in one of my books that will serve as an excuse for his generous assertion, but until then, alas, I remain free to deny my participation. And what is more important, I remain equally free to praise this courageous and remarkable attempt.

But we are dealing here with something more than an attempt. For years, preparatory work has been done with the greatest care. Certain signs of this work still cling to the œuvre presented. But I don't intend to analyse this under a magnifying glass, nor 'explicate' it. To criticize it would be much too easy. That I will do perhaps when Mr Decroux's work has become more familiar to me. For the moment it is enough to insist on the fact that if, during the performance, I was only once swept away by my enthusiasm, I was no less constantly convinced that I was seeing a serious attempt to create an art for the theatre. (We use the word *art* too lightly. We would not do so if we could find another to replace it.) I would not go so far as to say positively that this art was original – even though I am practically convinced of it – but I can swear to this: Mr Decroux has progressed towards such an art, he has walked without fear in the right direction, with a ferocious faith. That, we realized, had certainly been accomplished, and the ensemble was perfectly wonderful.

'Not more than that?' you will ask.

Yes, a great deal more. We were present at the creation of an alphabet, an ABC of mime. Or, if you refuse to allow the word 'creation', let's say 'rediscovery', since a rediscovery is indeed, don't you agree, the most we can accomplish? Treasures lie at our feet, here and there. We must accustom our eyes to see the enchanted seed, our ears to hear the mystic sounds.

I have travelled a great deal in Europe, visiting many cities in Holland, Germany, Russia, Italy, England, Scotland, but until now I had never seen anything comparable to this attempt.

You must not do me (and my subject) the injustice of supposing that I have used the work 'attempt' three times in order to diminish the work. I do not at all use it to this end, but only to avoid exaggeration in order to keep you – those of you who attended the performance with me – from shouting 'Bravo' too quickly the next time. For there exist among us a good number of incredulous ones – 'untouchables' – whom the grace of a huge tree does not impress, nor the strength of an ant. And we would like to see these sceptical friends convinced, moved and shouting 'Bravo!' Without them, the victory is only half won. So, the next time, give them the opportunity to acclaim Decroux a moment before you do.

For my part, I am entirely convinced by what I saw on 27 June of this year of liberation. Next to the work of Decroux and Barrault, the operas and other state theatres of Europe seem ridiculous. Anything but liberated, 'bound hand and foot' would be a better term for describing them.

Even assuming that one cannot stick the label of 'original' onto the work of Mr Decroux – but tell me, what is 'original' – what can be original? Mr Decroux could, for all I know, have seen years ago some Japanese toy and been inspired by it. Or else been inspired by some grandiose fragments of sculpture. No doubt, some traveller will come back some day from the icy zones of the far North to tell us that he saw, in Alaska, or in Iceland, people whose appearance reminded him over and over of Decroux, Barrault and Guyon in *Passage of Men Across the Earth*. I doubt it, by the way. But what importance would that have?

Mr Dalcroze, the collaborator of Adolphe Appia, perhaps already started the composition of an ABC of mime. Maybe he already got to the letter D. Mr Dorcy did not name Mr Dalcroze but he should not pass unnoticed. As for Isadora – inimitable and always imitated – she surely understood mime without even needing to invent an ABC. For there exists something incalculable, genius – always remember this – which has nothing to do with talent. For example, when Mr Barrault, that evening of 27 June, performed 'The Horse' for us, he did it by the grace of genius. And if the dissatisfied can't forgive him for it: too bad for them. Genius is something other than talent. You French people know that, but I will cite an English definition which I like: 'Genius arrives at its goal by instinctive perception and spontaneous activity, rather than by methods which allow for a well-defined analysis, and which are the methods that talent uses.'

This is completely Jean-Louis. Is it also Mr Decroux? I would be tempted to believe that Mr Decroux possesses genius but that, being a very wary man, he does not dare count on it *entirely* – he mistrusts it. He prefers to help his genius rather than to own it and enjoy it. They say he will come to be seen as the master of mime. I consider that the title already belongs to him.

Young people will read this article – it is especially dedicated to them, as I honour their enthusiasm – and as they already have (as I do) great admiration for what Mr Decroux does, they will be careful not to argue among themselves. Arguments may be good for those who hold political discussions but they cannot serve *us* in any way. We serve on the battlefield of art, and if we can't do something valuable, we must follow our leaders with great faithfulness. I followed mine – you will read someday the French translation of a book that I wrote to celebrate the memory of my teacher, Henry Irving. Disciples often want to teach things to their teachers. I didn't do that. I don't do it. Be careful, then, that your enthusiasm does not degenerate into selfishness. You would certainly not want to make Mr Decroux's task more difficult than it already is. But this is what you will do if you do not unite to support him, him and his idea (and not your own conception of his idea), to help him accomplish this idea. At his side, to help him, Jean-Louis Barrault – actor, director and creator of the most purely lyrical thing I have had the pleasure of seeing on stage up to this point: I mean 'The Horse'. Like all lyrical creation, large or small, this was easy to understand . . . and it was irresistible. You recognized it yourselves, as you shouted, applauded and made the most cheerful noise I've heard in years. And what did Barrault do? He made a simple inclination of the head – he did not want to come forward to bow, and bow again, and thus cause more applause. That is the attitude of an actor of rare quality and an exceptional man. Hold the memory of it dearly.

And, if you can, and are willing, know that I am sincerely your friend.

The hidden master

Eugenio Barba

[Reprinted from *Mime Journal: Words on Decroux 2*, 1997, translated from the Italian by Antonello Villani.]

It may be hard to believe that I first heard about Etienne Decroux in 1966 in Holstebro, Denmark, where the Odin Teatret had just moved from Norway. Maybe I had, in some of my readings, come upon his name, but it had not made a lasting impression. The elusive nature of the name Decroux makes one aware of one of the great injustices of theatre in our century.

Decroux began erecting the cathedral of Corporeal Mime at the close of the 1920s. He had personally known Copeau, taught at Dullin's school and collaborated with Artaud. He never stopped working. In 1940, he opened his mime school in Paris. Two of his pupils and collaborators, Jean-Louis Barrault – whom he had met in 1931 – and Marcel Marceau, became world famous. In 1963, the prestigious publisher Gallimard put out his book *Paroles sur le mime (Words on Mime)*.

In spite of it all, I knew nothing about Decroux even though I had been a student at the Warsaw Theatre School and had worked with Grotowski, and, as a self-taught man of the theatre, always hunted after the works of the masters and devoured French books. Though maybe I am to blame for the oversight, the name Decroux hardly ever surfaced at that time, and the tremendous value of what he had discovered and accomplished was not perceived as one of the theatre's great treasures. For me – as for Grotowski back then – the art of mime seemed to find its incarnation in the celebrated Marceau or in Lecoq.

It was Ingemar Lindh, a young Swede who had attended the mime classes Decroux taught in his own Paris home, who first told me about him. Ingemar illustrated the basic principles of the work done there and demonstrated some of the exercises he had learned. He told me many anecdotes revealing his master's personality. He also told me that he and some fellow students from Decroux's school wished to start a group but had no place to do it. I mentioned that if they agreed to live far from the world's theatre capitals they could settle in Holstebro and use the Odin Teatret space. That's how Ingemar Lindh, Yves Lebreton, Maria Lexa and Giselle Pellissier came to Odin Teatret in Holstebro, where they created Studio 2 in January 1968.

They were totally independent, making a kind of theatre that was profoundly different from ours. And yet we were both interested in each other's approach and shared a common attitude towards our work, a comparable way to reconcile anarchy and self-discipline. Decroux became a household name at Odin Teatret. I started thinking of him as a hidden master.

Etienne Decroux himself came to Odin Teatret in April 1969, when I invited him to a week-long seminar devoted to 'scenic language'. The two other guests were Jacques Lecoq and Dario Fo. Each presented his theatre works and rehearsal techniques and ran hands-on workshops with the Scandinavian actors and directors who took part in the programme. Decroux wore black shorts and a black tee shirt. Ingemar Lindh translated from the French into Swedish.

Sentences such as 'Le style c'est l'homme' (Style makes the man) and 'people stink' had the effect of bombs at a time in history that's etched in memory simply as 1968. But Decroux was not one to make concessions to political correctness. He was a proletarian and an anarchist, but he was also an aris-tocrat. He did not merely teach the 'scientific' principles of acting, but a way to *position oneself* which from posture and movement radiated to an all-embracing ethical and spiritual stance.

At the conclusion of the seminar, he presented me with a copy of his *Paroles sur le mime* (*Words on Mime*) with a friendly dedication. I have since read it over and over again, and it has become one of the sources I use to test the principles of Theatre Anthropology which I began outlining in 1980.

Earlier in 1969 I travelled to Paris to finalize Odin Teatret's participation in the Théâtre des Nations, and paid

Decroux a visit for the purpose of inviting him to the above-mentioned seminar. He and his wife gave me a warm welcome and we had a long chat in their small drawing room. I told them that we would bring our production, *Ferai*, to Paris the following summer and invited them to come and see it. Ingemar Lindh and Yves Lebreton shook their heads, as Decroux was no longer in the habit of going to the theatre.

However, when Odin Teatret arrived in Paris in June, Decroux and his wife surprisingly showed up at the *Ferai* premiere. The show was designed for an audience of no more than sixty on two rows of facing benches. The scenic space on which the actors operated consisted of the floor between the two rows. No sooner had Decroux sat down than he began voicing to his wife his reactions to such an unusual set-up. Decroux's critical grumbling did not end when the show began. On the contrary, it grew denser as it progressed. Then the man sitting next to him leaned over and whispered in his ear: 'Pardon, monsieur, mais vous dérangez le spectacle!' (Excuse me, sir, you are disturbing the performance!) Decroux got up and disdainfully answered: 'Monsieur, c'est le spectacle qui me dérange!' (Sir, it's the performance that's disturbing me!) He took his wife by the arm and left, walking like a king through the imperturbable actors. He almost slammed the door as he walked out.

Though I never saw him again, his writings and words, and all that he was able to transmit to his pupils and, through them, to me, have continued to influence my thoughts on the actor's *presence*.

The laws of art are relative. Their value does not lie in whether they are right or truthful. They only work if embraced wholeheartedly. They create a contradiction in that, while not absolute, they must be followed as though they were. This results in a paradoxical use of intolerance. Many masters of classic Asian theatre do not tolerate their pupils getting some of their learning from other sources. Sometimes they even forbid them to attend performances executed in a different style. In that, Decroux was the most 'Asian' of the European masters.

But, unlike the real world, where intolerance is used to destroy diversity, in the art world – and especially in the theatre – intolerance is a pedagogical fiction, as fictive as it seems ruthless. It is not used to destroy diversity, but to protect it and ensure its evolution. It has nothing to do with power and imposition, but with self-discipline and a refusal to compromise. That is why Decroux never accepted fluctuations of taste.

He loved poetry and the art of rhetoric. He was a great *raconteur*, yet he banned speech from mime, not out of personal distaste, but only to allow corporeal art to grow freely on its own, without what could have been the limiting intervention and mediation of language. This very particular form of artistic 'intolerance' was not unlike Craig's or Copeau's when they said that school rather than performance is the true objective of theatre, or Grotowski's, when he banned scenery, make-up and masks from his productions. This was not the product of a judgement, but of a strategy. Decroux used to talk a lot to his pupils as they learned the actions and movements of mime. He often made them sing or he sang to them. I wonder if he did it as a way to stress that in mime silence is like a vow of poverty that his pupils had to practise before they could give life to the *silence* of the body.

My last image of Decroux in his final months is both glorious and horrible. It is an indirect image which came to me through the eyes and words of his Brazilian pupil, Luis Octavio Burnier, a young director and teacher at the University of Campinas who had often worked with me both at the International School of Theatre Anthropology and during Odin's South American tours. He died in February 1995 of sudden cardiac arrest in the hospital where he was under observation for a backache.

'Decroux constantly sang at work,' Luis Octavio told me. 'The speed of each movement was dictated by the rhythm, while its dynamic quality was set by the intensity of the master's voice. Sometimes he sang alone while giving us directions. Other times we sang with him while practising. He picked old popular French and English tunes, which he interpreted with irony and with a distorted accent. Contrary to generally accepted rules, the breathing out was the active phase where he placed and developed the action. The breathing in was fast, and he called it *spasme*. It marked the beginning of the action which was intended to clash with the resistance obtained by stretching the breathing out as far as it would go.' And, Luis Octavio added, 'Decroux was obsessed with what he considered the invisible movement. He used the violin analogy. Sound can be heard even though the bow moves imperceptibly, so there is music even in the apparent absence of movement. He called it the gong effect. Like an echo, which lingers on, a movement continues even after it's completed.'

Decroux sang one last time for himself and his pupil when the latter paid him a visit in 1990. The master was in an armchair, staring into space, his mouth hollow without his dentures. When he saw his former pupil reaching out to hug him, he began to sing. He bounced his head from side to side and rolled his eyes, his mouth wide open as though trying to hold the final note of a line. In that, Luis recognized the 'violin effect'. Though the old man's body was paralysed and close to the end, Luis could feel his fingers rhythmically clutching his hand as though following a tune. The master lifted his forearm and elbow from the armrest and moved them with the sound. Luis, too, sang. The two sang together for over an hour. It was an extraordinary way to celebrate silence.

'He had a lion within,' Luis concluded, 'which only his technique could control.'

Decroux had his own peculiar way of speaking subliminally. For him, technique and ethics were one, so, whenever he illustrated some of the principles of mime art, he seemed to indicate a way to position oneself not only on the floor, but also in relation to life. In other words, for him, mime art and the art of living were one and the same. Thus, those who worked with Decroux learned more from him than technique alone.

One may say that still to this day Decroux is a hidden master, one who reveals himself in his own pupils. It is a great pleasure to meet them. They all seem to belong to the same clan, as though they had all been given the same set of values to share, values I share with them.

L'Homme qui voulait rester debout (The Man Who Preferred to Stand) was the title of a performance that some of his pupils dedicated to him in Philadelphia in early April

1992, a year after Decroux's death. In it, Steven Wasson and Corinne Soum reconstructed some of the master's works, including popular pieces such as *Le Combat antique* and *Le Menuisier*.

Decroux created these two pieces in 1945 and 1931. He continued teaching at his school until the beginning of 1987. In essence, if we consider his artistic incubation, and the work of discovery and invention begun at the time of his apprenticeship with Copeau, we could look at Decroux's as a teaching career that spanned a whole century.

Was it really an injustice that Decroux should remain unknown to so many? It was certainly unfair that the French government, so proud of its cultural institutions and so prone to bestowing honours and staging solemn ceremonials, never considered Decroux one of its glories. It isn't unfair, however, that his fame is not widespread. I believe that was a conscious choice on his part. Hundreds of people, actors and acting teachers all over the planet, were clearly imprinted by Decroux. One could even turn the fairness issue around and say that Decroux was the most influential of teachers, the only one to closely resemble the great masters of classic Asian theatres, who believed, just as he did, that it is impossible to separate doctrine from tradition, personal disposition, anger, humour, gentleness or sternness.

Taped excerpts of Etienne Decroux's voice were inserted between different acts of the performance in his honour produced one year after his death. His voice was endowed with a self-contained authority and the *grandeur* of those nineteenth-century anarchist labourers who spoke like kings.

The Decroux pupils I have met here and there in the world at different times since 1966 all share the distinction of being the children of an unknown king. Some of them are proud legitimate princes; others are secretly loved bastards. Still others are rebellious and disowned children – or so they feel – waiting for a chance to come home, while others freely dispense a knowledge Decroux himself would never have wanted, polluted by the need to make it public. Yet they all are the children of an anarchist king who himself was the son of an anarchist.

I was the guest in Philadelphia in early 1992, as though Decroux himself had secretly invited the stranger who had invited him in 1969. *A Tribute to Etienne Decroux*, an event sponsored by Movement Theatre International, was organized by Michael Pedretti. There I met some of the Decroux pupils and associates I had already heard about, such as Thomas Leabhart, Daniel Stein, George Molnar, Kari Margolis and Dulcinea Langfelder.

If I start counting from Ingemar Lindh and Yves Lebreton, all the way to the most recent Decroux pupils such as Eugenio Ravo and Michele Monetta, whom I met in occupied factories in Bologna and Naples, I realize that his pupils are like a tribe. Is it appropriate then to talk of him as a hidden master?

The theatre group founded by Steven Wasson and Corinne Soum, who are continuing Decroux's teaching tradition in London and created the Philadelphia production of the master's old and new pieces, is known as *L'Ange fou (The Crazy Angel)*. I wonder if there ever was a crazy angel of the theatre in this century, and, if so, who it is or was?

Decroux is the bridge between the generation of Craig and Copeau – their research and revolution – and those who, in the second half of this century, rediscovered the theatre as space and vehicle of paradox and rebellion.

In the theatre of our century, he stands out as a model who preserved his own *raison d'être* and tenacity, his unwavering commitment, with no need or inclination for alibis or compromises. He built a little island of freedom in his small house, and in the tiny room inside where he met with his pupils. He did not depend on anybody's financial support. There were times when he had very few pupils, but that did not persuade him to go in a different direction. His knowledge of the actor's pre-expressive level, how to build up *presence*, and how to articulate the transformation of energy, is unequalled in Western theatre history.

In my opinion, it is a tragedy that he was not equally obsessed with the creation and composition of productions, and that all his attempts were bound to an aesthetic philosophy that I do not believe capable of striking and moving an audience. I wonder if it was because he treasured research over everything else; or rather, because he truly believed, as Craig did, that it would be desirable to close down all theatres for many years and prepare to start again from the roots.

Finally, I wonder if Decroux's theatre was not after all made for a non-existent audience. Maybe if an angel dreamt like a madman, he would end up turning into such a man, such an actor and master.

Part two

Words of Decroux

1 Revolt

Figure 4 Etienne Decroux in *Sport* (c. 1948). Photographs by Etienne Bertrand Weill.

37

Figure 5 Etienne Decroux in *Sport* (c. 1948)

1.1 Corporeal mime and pantomime

[The text of a 1943 radio interview conducted by Christiane Fournier to 'establish a connection between the mime work of Etienne Decroux and the role he had just played in *Les Enfants du paradis*', translated from the French by Sally Leabhart.]

CHRISTIANE FOURNIER: *Mr Decroux, you must have been, I imagine, happy and in your element in your role.*

ETIENNE DECROUX: I was above all discreet, as the only role where one could show mime capabilities amply displayed was that of [Jean] Gaspard Deburau, played by Jean-Louis Barrault. My role came down to providing a foil for his.

CF: *Did you enjoy watching Barrault during the filming?*

ED: Tremendously. As much as I spurn the use of superlatives and other fancy words, I think that Barrault was light and energetic, and, if the public thinks as I do, they will see Barrault in his best role to date.

CF: *The pantomime in this film is historical. Can you tell us the difference you see between it and what you usually practise?*

ED: To answer you in a way that will not earn me a harsh reprimand from some erudite scholar hidden in the shadows, I would have to know the history of pantomime better than I do. Now, I am not an art historian. What time I have left over from my profession as an actor is taken up by the practice of mime and not by looking at the past or at Asia.

CF: *You won't get off the hook so easily. You must tell us something.*

ED: Let's go, then. I have at least a vision of old-style pantomime.

First of all, when I was still a child, I was fortunate enough to see pantomime's final tremors. Subsequently, I saw, as everyone has, engravings that depicted pantomimists at work. Then again, my intuition tells me that the mimed ballets at the Opéra [de Paris], and the acting styles of people who call themselves mimes, must contain some vestiges of the old-style pantomime. Finally, I have, after all, read a bit on the question.

First point: the face was nude and the body covered. I want the body to be nude and the face veiled.

CF: *There you have, indeed, a reversal.*

ED: As a consequence of this first point: [in old-style pantomime] the face had the leading role and the body limited itself to going along with it and prolonging its intentions without betraying them.

My taste is for the body to have the leading role, and the face, if it must be uncovered, is limited to going along with the body, prolonging its intentions without betraying them.

CF: *The reversal is complete. And why do you have such a low regard for the face and a high one for the body?*

ED: In my opinion, acting with the body is infinitely more poetic than acting with the face.

CF: *The face is nevertheless more expressive.*

ED: That's what I have against it. It's a material that is too easily worked, a body part which is too obedient. Great art implies rebellious matter. Now, the body is rebellious. Without imagining acrobatic or choreographic feats – without requiring oneself to become a serpent-man, if only to stylize the ordinary evolution of mankind – one must work for about ten years. And this does not do away with the necessity of having talent and culture.

But the area of difficulty is necessarily that of noble art. Beauty does not give her favours at the first request, she wants proof of love.

Moreover, if the face is expressive, it does not take us to a different world. If it gets to that other world, it is because it is impassive and mummified, becoming mask-like, and that brings us to Corporeal Mime. When the body acts, carrying its face, one should be able to say [of the face] these two verses of Hugo [from 'L'Aigle du casque'].

Qui paraissait rêver au centre d'une toile,
Pas plus ému d'un choc que d'un souffle une étoile.

[Who seemed to be dreaming in the center of a canvas,
No more fearful of a blow than would be a star of a puff of air.]

The nude body expressing what one receives generally from words and from the gaze, transports us to another world.

The face sweats reality. And there is even something immodest in using such an intimate part of the body to cry in front of everyone. The movements of the soul are private things. To show one's nude body is not the same as showing one's inner life. In love, for example, it is verifiable that if there is lewdness somewhere, it is found in the face. If I were a woman I would be less embarrassed to be a prostitute than to be an actress. I would like the actor not to be a man deprived of a private life, that he be a real person as are the sculptor, the painter, the composer. But the best reason for my preferring the body is that face re-presents and the body creates.

The face presents a second time what it presents a first time in life. It produces for everyone the sadness it felt on its own. It's realism. For art to exist, one must create. The body can create: professions mould the body. So much so that there are bent-over men, others as straight as sticks and others bearing the mark of having been mixed.

It's been ages since man expressed states of his soul with his body. The result is that if today he intended to do so, he would have to devote himself to serious study.

CF: *Don't you run the risk of lacking artists beautiful enough to practise this art?*

ED: Beauty in the proportions is not required so much. Movement erases forms. What Baudelaire said about movement in relation to the beauty of forms he could have said about the ugliness of forms.

Unlike the face, the body is large; its parts cover large distances. In art, moral grandeur implies physical grandeur. A fresco is worth more than a miniature. The word *knick-knack* [*chinoiserie*] has a pejorative meaning. In miniature, even if it were well-modelled, the Arc de Triomphe would not be worth much. Certain of Rodin's famous works were reproduced in small scale; they were thereby impoverished. In the Middle Ages, some cathedrals, the day of their inauguration, collapsed. If they had been little, the fatal flaw in their construction would have remained unnoticed.

Physical size is not moral greatness; while not the cause of greatness, it is, however, a condition for it. Large things are not always imposing, but imposing things are always large.

With pantomime before him, the spectator feels condescending. He is crushed by sculpture, troubled by painting, exhausted by music and respectful of theatre.

Mime must inspire in him the same consideration. It must be a *didascalos* [teaching play], serious and captivating, and not a childish diversion. To do that it must seem to live for itself, and not seem to explain itself.

CF: *What do you think of theatre?*

ED: I think that it is an excellent literature for people who don't know how to read; that the actor prevents us from imagining the hero, in his true glory, that [the actor] wants to bring back to life.

CF: *Will the art of mime succeed in becoming as intelligible as speaking theatre is?*

ED: To ensure this we must give it the same means: the same number of actors, the same talent in each actor and a residence as prolonged in mime as in the theatre.

CF: *Supposing your art absolutely ready, do you hope it will be popular?*

ED: The general public prefers an orator to a writer and an athlete to an accountant – they like heroes to prove their hearts with their muscles. They don't like overwrought texts very much.

CF: *If one imagines the beauty of mime, we have trouble imagining that it can be varied. Wouldn't it be monotonous?*

ED: When I was little I couldn't understand that one could discover a new melody without stumbling into an already known one. Believe me, if one managed to control each part of his body as one wanted to, this body would offer us infinite combinations.

CF: *As soon as one seeks to make of the art of mime no longer a show for a particular occasion, whose success comes perhaps from the special talents of the individual performer who gives himself over to it, as soon as one wants to have the art of mime become the foundation of one's theatrical work, a regular show, this question presents itself: will the average artist be able to practise this art form?*

ED: I think so, because the greater the number of mimes on stage, the less genius each one needs. It is easier to perform a speaking play [with many actors] than it is for a lone actor to hold the stage for an entire evening with a series of poems. Mime is impossible so long as one refuses to do it, but not when one resolves to do it.

CD: *Can you speak to us about the training of a mime artist?*

ED: He must assimilate a special physical education. He must contemplate works of the art of drawing. He must get a certain musical training in order to make music flow in the veins of his muscles, and not in order to spread it around himself. The study of diction will be for him the beginning of the art of autosuggestion.

CD: *In short, for you, one must be an actor before being a mime.*

ED: Yes.

[The following notes are of further ideas offered for the interview, but which were not used.]

– A painting of a mime performance:

Nude actor, bare stage, silence – nothing 'up one's sleeve'. An emotion comparable to that provoked by the imagined materialization of occultism, and this created by the suggestion of physical things. A narrator would say the nouns.

Figure 6 Figures 6, 7 and 8 Etienne and Maximilien Decroux in November 1947 in *Ancient Combat*. Photographs by Etienne Bertrand Weill.

– If music must be included, it should come in only after the mime work is finished.

Creation: 1. Intelligibility
             2. Stylization
             3. Rhythm in various places
             4. Harmonizing of individual rhythms among
               themselves
             5. Music

– One must banish mime conventions and attempts to explain using mime, and replace them with words, spoken or written.

1.2 The method

[Translated from the French by Sally Leabhart.]

There is one method directed by the mind and another by circumstance. When I imagine that I am director of a dramatic arts convent, where the students wouldn't have anything other to do except learn their profession and where I would not have anything else to do but teach them, I would adopt the following as spiritual rules:

1. Teach the art of speaking along with gymnastics. Thus, exclude for a short while the study of mime, at first. Since for modern man, words were the most natural method of expression, the art of feeling and expressing must thus begin by the study of texts.

   This life set in motion by the word tends to spill over into the body, and if that spilling over of life into the body very quickly comes to an end, it's because of the inability of the actor. The actor's body is a corked still in which life, poured in at the top, has no chance of circulating. Gymnastics not only allows one to do what one imagines – to continue, however one wants, a movement already begun; gymnastics has, in addition, the virtue of suggesting movement figures.

   A student who never studied mime, and who limited his studies to diction and gymnastics, would know three-quarters of mime.

2. Ask the student to accomplish, including in the following order: corporeal mime, vocal mime, facial mime, through artistic expression, equally mastered and to arrive thereby at speaking theatre.

General attitude for the Method

Give up trying to make a name for oneself in the theatre and film, as the obligations of this kind of life are more harmful than the benefits of prestige and material means they provide. All of this diverts us from the goal and puts off the task indefinitely. Prestige and material means are precious, but they cost too much to acquire.

Steps for finding sleeping partners, subsidies, official appointments, outstanding roles, etc., take all one's time and also occupy too much of one's thought. One must turn one's back on salons, on committees, on casting cafes, on utilitarian friendships . . .

Give up all reformist methods. That is to say, those which consist of inserting mime into verbal plays. This heresy only discredits mime, guilty of stopping the verbal rhythm. Moreover, it confuses the issue and prevents one from assessing progress.

Refuse any mime lessons to anyone who will not agree to undertake three years' study of gymnastics.

Refuse to put on mime performances without mimes – that is to say, putting a dancer here, a speaker there, a singer in one place and a group of gymnasts in another, adding in

Figure 7 Maximilien and Etienne Decroux in *Ancient Combat,* November 1947.

theatrical lighting, and all of it pasted onto a work of literature.

There is more fundamental mime in the diction of a Lucien Guitry [French actor 1860–1925] than in the gesticulations of a student in a youth hostel [cultural centre] or in the cabrioles of a dancer.

1.3 From the personality of Etienne Decroux...

[Written early 1948, translated from the French by Sally Leabhart.]

... a pronounced taste stands out for:

1. Bodily movement (sport, dance, circus)
2. Statuary and architecture
3. Rhyming poetry
4. Philosophy or explication
5. The nation (politics, religion)

as well as an absence of: a need for music for music-lovers; of painting; of novels; of jewellery; of archaeology for itself; country life; the spectacle of Nature;

a hostility towards mystery;

a disinterest for everything which, because it speaks of private life and personal views, does not lead towards universal man, towards the salvation of humankind.

From his Professional Activity, the following stands out:

1. From the age of thirteen to twenty-five: manual worker (masonry, plumbing, roofing, butchery, hospitals, wagon factory, restaurants, etc.).

   Having become an artist, he returned to his former profession of roofer for several summers, periods when his theatre was closed.

2. Then, he becomes an actor in the theatre and in film, on the radio and television.
3. Little by little, he distances himself from these things while becoming more and more engrossed in the following things, to the point of making a new profession out of them: lectures on the philosophy of fine arts, public reading of poetry and the art of mime.

In each one of these branches, he works against the main-stream.

In lectures: against the arts of mixing.

In poetry readings: against the custom of reducing the diction of verse to that of prose.

In the practice of mime: against the use of the face and hands as instruments of expression.

1.4 Autobiography of Etienne Decroux

[Written early 1950 prior to his tour of Israel; translated from the French by Sally Leabhart.]

Childhood

For a long time, my father took me every Monday to the musical variety show that was known as the Café-Concert.

This father built houses with his hands.

He involved me in prolonged discussions about the just and the unjust. In our neighbourhood, he was the only one to have the ideas he had.

He frequented a family of Italian sculptors.

He washed my body in a completely natural way, prepared food, painted my throat [when I was ill] and, pensively, cut my hair.

Sometimes, in restrained tones, he read poetry to me.

So that none of his gestures might serve as a bad example, he watched himself. Thus he refused to shake the hand of a friend when [this friend] was drunk, because I was there.

A nest blocked the rain gutter. He built a cage without a door, and hung it very high because of the cats. The sparrows were moved in without having to leave their bed. He put bird feed beside them, and the bird-parents came into the cage to carry out the service.

When the first circus that I had ever seen left town, I must have been secretly crying. My father guessed as much, I think, for he caressed my heart with his voice.

I looked at my father as one looks at a moving statue.

Thus: Music Hall, Morality, Heresy, Poetry, Pantheism, Circus, Sculpture and Fatherhood leading the soul back to its roots. . .

And that is how I became cultivated.

Youth

Until my twenty-fifth year, I worked mostly in construction, but I took on a lot of other things.

I remember having been a painter, plumber, mason, roofer, butcher, navvy, dock worker, wagon repairman, dishwasher, nurse. I even placed rubber hermetic seals on freezer doors. I made hay and harvested grain. You must not forget that in 1917 I was a second-class soldier for three years. You can imagine that in all the jobs I mentioned I was always third class.

Even so, there were plenty of things to see!

There are unfortunate people who have not seen anything of all this.

I wonder how they manage to put a play on stage.

These things, seen and even handled, have passed, little by little, to the back of my head, made their way down the back of my arms and arrived at the ends of my fingers where they changed my fingerprints.

I enjoyed myself. I saw old-style pantomime, still alive and above all hardy, and its grimaces made me do likewise. I saw sports. I saw in it the original form of dramatic art. I was nearly bowled over with admiration for it. Finally I attended a play. It struck me as being an art form that walked on its feet while looking up into the air.

And that is how I became exalted.

Vocation

At twenty-five, having saved enough to live a year without salary, I entered Jacques Copeau's school. The echoes of Gordon Craig's theories had reached it. There, students, with nude bodies, faces veiled, composed scenes without words.

And that's how I got pointed in a certain direction.

Apprenticeship

At twenty-seven, having spent time with [Gaston] Baty's [1885–1952] and [Louis] Jouvet's [1887–1951] theatres, I joined the theatre of [Charles] Dullin [1885–1949] for eight consecutive years.

And that's how I got adjusted.

Profession

I acted in twenty-some films, took up my position at each microphone and took speaking theatre pieces around [France] on the train.

And that is how I got bored.

Early career

In the theatre, I had some success as Tchernozium in [Valentin Petrovich Kayayev's 1928 farce about Soviet marriage and housing conditions] *The Squaring of the Circle*; as Trotsky in [François Porché's 1931 play] *The Tsar Lenin*; and Captain Smith in *Captain Smith*.

In films, I had some success as the hat thief in [Pierre and Jacques Prévert's 1932] *L'Affaire est dans le sac*; as the father of Debureau in [Marcel Carné and Jacques Prévert's 1945] *Les Enfants du paradis*; and as the Balkan conspirator in [Pierre Prévert's 1947] *Voyage surprise*.

And that's how I thought I had taken off.

School director

I studied the art of theatre like no one ever has before. I devoured books and practised with the physical commitment of a manual labourer.

I always wanted to test beauty by reason alone. I was obliged to analyse figures which I taught students so that they could repeat them.

Little by little, I built up not only a doctrine but a pedagogy.

In the theatrical tribe my classes quickly became famous and attended by only a few. Everyone came to me and left as easily. Among the names known in France, [actor and director] Jean-Louis Barrault [1910–94], [pantomime] Marcel Marceau [1923–2007], [actress] Maria Casarès [1922–96], [and Parisian theatre directors and company founders Jean-Pierre] Grenier and [Olivier] Hussenot attended my school.

And that is how I became limited.

Troupe director

Slowly but surely, things fell into place.

We gave performances of pure Corporeal Mime in the biggest venues in Paris: Palais Chaillot, Sarah Bernhart [now Théâtre de la Ville], [Salle de] Chimie, Cité Universitaire.

In Belgium, we performed outside France for the first time; in Switzerland, we did two tours in the same season.

And now we are negotiating with [sponsors in] the USA.

In the meantime, we are on Israeli soil, full of History, full of the Future, where the Jews who are constructing their autonomous state welcome actors who are building theirs.

51

Doctrine

The theatre will only be worthy of its name when those who act refuse to obey those who write.

First, one must improvise without even knowing the subject.

Thus: find a theme, then a second, then a third.

One must, therefore, act in order to think.

Figure 8 Etienne and Maximilien Decroux in November 1947 in *Ancient Combat*

By putting into a logical order the ideas found in moving, a play takes form without any word breaking the silence.

One finds the usefulness of words in doing without them.

One will see that they serve some purpose, and that they do not serve much purpose.

Little by little, decade after decade, a truly new dramatic art will arise as a tree grows, with the same slowness, with the same richness and as lasting.

I have done things. Others will do them better, indefinitely . . . so long as I have done them well enough to put forward the idea that others will be able to do them better.

Bodily Presence

[Article originally published in *La Revue Esthétique*, March 1960; translated from the French by Sally Leabhart. The French title, 'Presencé en corps', could be a pun, 'en corps' sounding like 'encore'. The entire article, furthermore, rich in poetic alliteration and rhythm, often stretches grammatical rules.]

> One doesn't write on human skin the way one writes on parchment.
>
> (Catherine of Russia)

To have only his body as his material is for the artist a striking condition. The body is in fact remarkable and impossible to pulverize. It's a pity. The advantage would be clear if, without killing this body, one managed to reduce it to powder or to carve it up into tiny cubes. These parts, too small to interest the eye, too uniform as well, would be arranged as one wished; then one would reveal to the world the arrangement of these specks concealed from the world's view.

No one is distracted from a painting by its 'molecules' of colour and even the freestones don't distract us from the monument. You fortunate brothers of mosaic, of sculpture in stone or bronze, or glass, who have at your disposal unremarkable particles, sometimes even invisible to the attentive gaze, and moreover all of them alike.

The atom is the infantry soldier of the fine arts, except for mime. The parts of the body are very far from being particles. They differ from each other, we identify them; each of them as they show themselves announces its function to us; they are already completed works, they have a human shape.

If creating means making something out of nothing, these things are quite troubling, for they are not nothing. The mime's body seems to be something original intended to be a portrait. Thus we will only see the extra-human world through this human body. We will only see other men's bodies through one actor's body. We will only see the general through the particular, the abstract through the concrete, the future and the past through the present, the hidden via what is shown, thought via the thinker.

And so: gas, rays, fire, colours, vegetal things, intentions, minerals, woman or child's body, obese ones, long thin ones, things that grow, things that crawl or fall through the sky [*tombe sur le ciel*, literally, 'fall on the sky'] an amputee and hunchback, things that last by living on through what succeeds them, things that imagine they are unique and live only as a plural, will be represented by the body of an actor as specific, as inharmonious, as inflexible as an ordinary man's. To whom do we assign the responsibility of distracting one's gaze away from the unfortunate form, unfortunate because it is immobile in just the place it should be offering variety through change? Who will make stone seem to flow?

Movement takes on this mission because it moves lines from place to place. But this body, unable to change its form, is it only able to make movements other than its own?

Our body is behind our eyes. That's how things begin. Let's consider what happens next. Thought is egalitarian and the body is not. If, even with this body, we only intended to represent the physical position and movement of our own body, artistically speaking, one obstacle would remain: the audience's demand is that this body move evenly in space and time, whereas in this body the demand is to move only unevenly.

In saying this, I am not referring to the fact that this body doesn't articulate in all directions, at the knee and at the elbow, that we don't have eyes in the back of our head . . . that our spine is not in the middle of our trunk. If, through grace, this evenness were granted to us as soon as we walked on stage, it would be a burdensome gift.

Poetry is a thought for absent things. And yet the body is present. Art is an echo, a tamed accident, an arrhythmia in the aquarium of rhythm. Like those large brass vases embellished by the engraver, the body is 'fired and fired again'. It has, if it exists, something of ceramic pottery. But the body, on the other hand, is raw and therefore able to rot. It sweats; the effort it seems to make, it is making it for real; its sperm is on stage with it. Thus, when this body represents only itself, it's already too much.

If the mime solves these problems, it will prove itself of great merit. If it doesn't solve them at all, it still has one merit: that of being an ethical example. The mime does what he thinks; he doesn't have someone else do it for him. The stones he has laid never hold on their own. The curved line that he conceives of from the ankle to the skull, going from the ground to the ground, it's his body that makes it and it's with his body. He's a surgeon who operates on himself, but without a mirror.

Concerning the solicitor who plays soccer, we can't say that his sport gives form to his profession. The mime's thought takes form in his body. It's only in physical pain that moral strength is felt.

I like the stone carver who must work directly with matter: that's someone who knows what a challenge it is to complete the word without overloading the writings; he feels the idea ready to make its way through a space whose distance is as yet unmeasured. But if I imagine this sculptor having become fabulously wealthy, what comes immediately to mind is the thought that he won't lose any sleep over a piece of ruined marble, whereas no amount of fortune will excuse the mime from making with his body the settling of an error and fulfilment of a promise.

Figure 9 and 10 These two snapshots of Decroux, one taken in the 1970s (unattributed) and the other in the 1980s (by Robert Pruzan), show a richly textured and carefully organized environment. The stacks of papers fastened with butterfly clips seem scarcely to have moved in a decade, yet like building blocks of a monument, he took them out, considering and revising each one, scribbled on them, enlarged and condensed them, and eventually carefully repositioned them to the left of his green felt ink blotter.

Mark Piper, former student of Decroux and translator of *Words on Mime*, writing about the stacks of paper, remembers them this way:

> My area was solely *le grand a* [the big or broad a]. Every day . . . I provided him with an English word, pronounced in British English with an open a, e.g. my own Christian name. He would read the word, listen to my pronunciation of it, generally mull it over in his inimitable way, comment on French words that this brought to his mind. This would take anything from five minutes to three-quarters of an hour(!). He filed away the small slips of paper upon which I penned these items of vocabulary and this could possibly account for some of the bundles you refer to. As to the rest, all I know about them is that he would occasionally gesture magisterially towards them and say that this represented some of the work he had done over the years on phonetics and philology. (I'm not at all sure how much of this research would stand rigorous academic scrutiny but, after all, he wasn't doing it for anyone but himself.) I remember that from time to time a pile might have found its way off the bookshelf and on to the table and I always

felt myself in close proximity to some arcane mysteries which I hoped he might initiate me into; alas, no such ceremony ever took place. (Email from Mark Piper to Leabhart, 20 March 2008)

In the first photograph, he wears a velour bathrobe (one of a small collection) over his black shirt and black boxing shorts. The books on French literature, sculpture, phonetics, etymology and politics line the wall to his right; he read almost nothing on theatre. We also see clearly in the first photograph, behind Decroux, the manuscripts (now presumed lost) he laboured over on etymology and Corporeal Mime. In the second photo we can see the door (with a curtain-covered window and oval porcelain knob) from the small kitchen into the study. To the left of the door we see, indistinctly, a sideboard protected by an oil-cloth.

The mime's thought passes through needles, slowly, in his flesh to embroider the figure that he is performing. In this world, some think without doing and others do without thinking; the former gives the order and the latter carries it out. That explains many things. The practice of mime exalts the meaning of responsibility. To do, oneself, what one is calling for: this is answering the call.

2 A new school

2.1 Creating a mime play

[From a lecture by Etienne Decroux, given at his school in the mid-1980s, first published in *Mime Journal* 2000–2001, translated from the French by Sally Leabhart.]

Figure 11 Etienne and Maximilien Decroux in March 1948. This photograph, taken in Decroux's study, shows his interest in literature, sculpture and masks. Photograph by Etienne Bertrand Weill.

I have created a few more than fifty pieces, sometimes presented in public.

A piece can last an hour and a half, or fifteen minutes, sometimes three minutes. It would be interesting to manage to speak of them without justifying them. Obviously it would be bad taste to say: 'it's a good piece'. I must at least try to tell you how the idea came about. That's what's interesting: how can one create a mime piece? The petri dish is improvisation, above all when you have good improvisers. There are good years for improvisation in the same way that there are good years for wine. There was one year around 1950 when the improvisations were so extraordinary that we invited guests each time. There was Marceau, who was brilliant, and others, who were truly brilliant. I never gave them a theme, I said: 'The session is open! Anyone who wants to go on to the stage, go!' They did what they liked. Another who was there would say: 'Well, I want to improvise, too' and it happened like that, without a theme beforehand. The theme grew out of the actions, which seemed to happen by chance.

I wrote (with a fountain pen) three mime plays. Even though I think in images, each one was a failure, and that was the proof that one should not sit down to write. I write my lectures after having given them. I have a certain carefully wrapped stash of lectures that I have given in different capital cities (Amsterdam, Stockholm, Oslo, etc.). They were written after they were given, after I had returned to Paris.

That's how one should make theatre pieces. One should write them after having rehearsed them. I say this for speaking theatre, but for mime it's the same thing. It must first of all function. I like this word very much. It is from an American whom the French like very much, Jack London. When one produces a mime play, it must function, and to be sure that it functions, there must be improvisations. But, there you have it; there is a resemblance between improvisation and life. Improvisation is a little bit like life, really, and life, as you know, is what happens in the street. How do we know, then, among the many things one sees in an improvisation, which should be retained? There's the question. The world is full of symbols, and must we discover what these symbols are?

Symbols of what? Symbols of interesting things. And if one does not know what an interesting thing is, how can one find out? When you go into the world, you are going to see injustices and disorder, and if that does not move you, what will you do? Generally, art is a complaint. Art is a protest. A happy man, one who feels that everything is going well, cannot be an artist. You must first have that, and if you don't have that, look for it in novels and perhaps in plays. There are ideas; try to see which ones can be translated into mime. And above all else, one must have a sense of justice and injustice. Even disorder is injustice. Basically, everything comes down to justice and injustice.

So, how does a piece come about? One must not forget that there is another factor in the construction of a piece: the association of ideas. For example, one year we did, strictly for pedagogical purposes, a study of movements along floor patterns. It was the year of floor patterns. We had the year of juggling, the year of acrobatics, the year of instrumental music. There is one madness per year. That was the year of walking, in a very ordinary way, following a geometric plan, to obtain a certain effect: the idea of a square, of a circle, the idea of the surface. Among these exercises there was one entitled Maximum Contradiction. It was a question of walking without stopping; to make two steps, then an acute angle, two steps more and an acute angle, etc., etc. It was very difficult. First I marked the pattern on paper, and then I marked it with chalk on the stage. The actor had to pass through this Maximum Contradiction. In appearing in these diverse angles, the actor was very interesting. Afterwards, there was a second actor who followed the first one, and when the first one appeared almost facing forward, the second appeared almost facing backward. We said, well, this could represent soldiers marching in formation. And that was the starting point! We said the word 'soldiers' and that was the start of *The Little Soldiers*. But we also had to represent the interior of the barracks, the soldiers on leave, the declaration of the war of 1914, and the war itself, and the death of the little soldiers. The piece lasted one and a half hours without lowering the curtain. We made it quite varied. It was not always the same style of acting.

So, on one hand, having a sense of the just and the unjust, discovering what symbolizes the just and the unjust, and then taking off from something, something which seems like nothing, and allowing yourself to be guided by an association of ideas. But there is, even so, something one could call orchestra, and for me, it was relatively easy. I was full of memories. I saw French patriotism before 1914, when war was going to be declared; I marched in the streets of Paris; and then there was the declaration of war. I was in Paris. I saw the soldiers and the reserves leave. Then I was a soldier myself and I saw the never-ending war firsthand. All that stayed with me. It made the construction of the piece easy.

2.2 The imaginary interview (or the maxims of Étienne Decroux)

[For his 2003 book, entitled *Etienne Decroux, mime corporel*, Patrick Pezin worked with interviews with Decroux, and lectures which Decroux gave in his school (recorded and transcribed by Thomas Leabhart, Claire Heggen and Yves Marc between 1968 and 1987, here translated from the French by Sally Leabhart). By cutting and pasting, Pezin grouped Decroux's words around specific topics, creating an imaginary interview which gives a clear idea of Decroux's thinking on key topics during those years.

The 'Words of Decroux' included in this section are not so much extracts from theoretical texts as transcripts of performance and performative texts and are more akin to modernist art manifestoes and poetry than much contemporary theory. The ellipses in the text are not there to indicate editorial excisions, but to document the breaks and silences of speech, the relationship between movement and stillness, the voice and the body, as in a dramatic text. The production of words always involves something other than words . . . Before any word is spoken the body is already there . . . and Decroux always reminds us of the primacy of the body in theatre.]

I Of the origins of mime and a conception of the world

What is the genesis of Corporeal Mime?

It's always difficult to know when something started (*laughs*). I can tell you that, yes indeed!

To begin with there is my father's character. He was a Savoyard, of modest, country origins, a farmer. When he left Savoy, he went all over the place: Chamonix, Lyons, Paris . . . He did all sorts of . . . – I don't call them jobs – . . . more like activities that enable one to earn a living. He was an extraordinary man. He had a sense of the political ideal. He was what we could call a *fouriériste*. He didn't know the name Charles Fourier [French utopian socialist, 1772–1837], but his political thoughts were close to what we call Fourier's phalanstery [a cooperative community]: the idea of a community. The descriptions he used were enticing and they had a decisive influence on me. I remain forever marked by what one could call political lyricism. Thanks to him, for me nothing is above a political sense. Even if I believed in God, I could manage somehow to fit Him into that purview.

Then, there is my nature. I am what you could call a materialist-spiritualist. That is to say that the spiritual influences me when it gives form to the material.

I remember having read in a newspaper something about a plan for the construction of a stadium in the United States whose feature was that it could hold tens of thousands of people. It was an extraordinary number. I was greatly moved by this idea, that there could be so many people sitting in one place, all watching the same spot. I found that moving.

And, in a similar vein, the foreign Francophiles who come to Paris, take home with them a miniature Eiffel Tower, a miniature Arc de Triomphe, a miniature of Rodin's *Thinker* and other things like that. But they're not beautiful! You're going to tell me that they're not beautiful because they're not precise reproductions. No! That's not the reason, even if the Eiffel Tower were to be reproduced in miniature in great detail, and Rodin's *Thinker* with perfect accuracy. No! It must be large. Great thoughts must be loud enough for everyone to hear. We don't whisper grand ideas to a friend; they have to be said to a people. It has to be audible, loudspeakers are needed, something that shouts the thing.

Obviously all of this stems, a little, from my socialist temperament. I have a taste for singing choirs, speaking choirs, processions, protests in chorus and, of course, I'm drawn to monuments because monuments are places where people come together. Each person sees the others, the others see each person, and I find that moving. Getting out of your petty self, leaving your petty habits, seems to me an immensely appealing thing, and it's the only thing that excites me. So, obviously, that brings me to this second idea: the idea must become material. That's why I liked sculpture; apart from my love for sculpture, I loved sports. I've always loved sports, because I saw in a physical form – I was going to say 'material form' – the human struggle. Things don't start to interest me until they become material. When you get down to it, I feel as if I am more Christian than it seems.

Maybe you know about that dispute in the Catholic Church over what mattered the most in God's eyes, faith or works. Well, for me, the two things are reconcilable in the following way: it's faith that counts, but it can only be proven by works. We need works in order to measure faith, to take it seriously. All of this is very significant, but does not yet give us mime. So, was I attracted to dance because it's dance that one could see? Not entirely. I was more attracted to statuary than to dance, because something about dance did not seem serious to me, something that seemed fluid, elusive, like a wave, and the fact that it didn't stop, it didn't settle, it didn't speak, it didn't articulate.

If I was attracted to almost all the arts – though unequally, but by all of them – nevertheless, there was one which I really disliked: old pantomime – that's what I call it – which was not yet dead, and a few of whose last performances I saw in the café-concerts. What gave it a renaissance, what extended its life, was the birth of cinematography. Since film was silent, there was a general call-up of everyone who had done mime and pantomime. There you have it. But I really liked silent films, despite the presence of people who had done pantomime. Pantomime for the stage, I detested it.

The latter was condemned to do certain unpleasant things in order to exist, but I did not see why it wanted to exist. Example: the lighting was dim. Performances were lit with candles, which means that one could not see the changing facial expressions – and that explains, in part, why mimes had their faces painted white, with black lines for emphasis. That explains, above all, why pantomimes had to have facial expressions that one can call extreme. In the prints depicting old pantomime, one always feels as if they are going from one extreme to the other. Surprise is intense, anger is intense, everything is intense and you get the feeling that it's fake. Fake in the sense that, by the way they performed, it seemed as if the pantomime wanted to use gestures to get across what words could easily explain. It was gesticulations, facial expressions, so that it was a comic art even before it began. It didn't need to treat a comic subject; it was already comic.

To show the contrary, take for example the photographic enlargement. Let's take Michèle Morgan and suppose that, for publicity purposes, we wanted to reproduce her face on the side of a skyscraper. In this case, we make the photograph almost as big as the building itself, and yet, it's not untrue. It's not untrue because the photographic enlargement enlarged everything at the same time. On the other hand, in pantomime, if we can't see your half-smile, they exaggerate things, and you're going to have to make a big smile. Consequently you are condemned to doing something false in order to be visible. What was a slight dissatisfaction is going to become a big dissatisfaction.

Also, there is the risk of being obscene. There is nothing more obscene than the face. The body is never as obscene as the face. I was a nurse for four years. I was in the operating room, and there I saw around three or four female genitals each day. And, I would say, even to their very depths. It had no effect on me one way or the other. Female genitals don't have anything extraordinary in terms of obscenity; they're genitals, that's all. The face is a strange thing. It's the receptacle of almost everything. If we take our five senses, we have sight, that's in the face, taste, it's in the face, hearing, it's in the face, smell, it's in the face, and touch also can be in the face ... whereas movements of the body can never have the obscenity of a face. Except ... except if the body is at rest. On that subject, I remember a little story. I was in New York and there was an actor, a very handsome actor at that, who was just beginning his improvisations with us and I see him in briefs, so almost naked, let's say naked. Because he was doubtless searching for something, an idea, or maybe he wanted to put himself in a certain state, the fact remains that he was relaxed and that made it look dreadful. He was standing on the stage a bit the way a speaking actor might stand at that, but where the difference was great is that a speaking actor says things before relaxing. When he relaxes his muscles, he says more things and the words inhabit the space. Words have duration, one can't ignore them; so that a speaking actor whose body is at rest will be able to say his text without it seeming abhorrent.

We're in the presence of two systems here: the muscular system and the glandular system. The glandular system can be represented by the act of eating, or the act of feeling sexual desire. The glandular system is the opposite of the muscular system which consists of tension. The glandular system needs rest.

If an actor is almost naked on stage and he is in a state of rest, he suggests to us the glandular system and consequently his stance is indecent, not to say obscene. We don't go to a performance to put ourselves in a glandular state but rather into an intellectual one, and thought, itself, is like a muscle. Thought resembles the muscular system when the former is truly muscular.

I am thinking of a country where Puritanism is still in fashion and where I've been told that if someone photographed me naked, that is to say in briefs, that photograph wouldn't appear in any newspaper. Of course, in this same country, these days, eroticism is in fashion. It's a fad like any other. It's a cold frenzy like any other. In this same country, they had boxing matches. And yet the boxers were naked, either really naked or almost naked. The shorts were unimportant. And by the way, when I started to perform, I wore shorts, and yet that did not disarm the journalist who said, 'If we photograph you like that, the picture won't appear in any newspaper.' If it's a boxer, they'll allow it, because the boxer is not in a glandular state, but a muscular one.

But I return to our pantomime. So, pantomime – this play of the face and hands that seems to explain things – and which seems unable to access speech, seemed to me ridiculous and indecent, precisely because it explained itself and I have a little bit the feeling that we only express ourselves well when we don't explain ourselves; there's one thing I'll say about it. I hated this form that seemed comic to me before we even knew what it was about. I thought that we should do something serious, that an art had the duty to be, first of all, serious. Art is firstly a complaint. Someone who is happy with things does not belong on stage. The day when everyone is happy, if that could happen, theatre will no longer exist. What I'm sure of is that I don't see how we can practise an art if it's not to depict our sufferings, our discontent.

To finish on this subject, it would be easy for me to make a distinction between old pantomime and our Corporeal Mime. We never saw the old pantomimes performing with their backs to the audience, while we, in *The Factory*, performed a great deal with our backs to the audience. I already told you, but I'll repeat it, we only express ourselves well when we don't explain ourselves. You have to be a hero without knowing it: the greatest pantomime in the world, with his face, would not be worth the back of a working fireman.

We say: Corporeal Mime. But what is the body?

The body: the first idea that comes is that it's neither the arms, nor the face.

We know full well that the face is part of the body and that the arms are part of the body, of course, but when we speak spontaneously we say: elbows against the body, arms around the body, etc. We make a distinction. The body is above all the trunk.

But the trunk itself is carried by the legs; so it is, above all, the trunk held up by the legs. Immediately, we feel our complete responsibility and our entire body is engaged. We feel that we might fall if we went to the edges of imbalance. It's very demanding and it doesn't lie.

With the body, it is very difficult to lie. It's understood that the body will necessarily assume shapes. Imagine a man who receives some very bad news. He goes home; he is alone in his bedroom. We can imagine his comportment, even without looking through the keyhole, and we presume that his spine is going to collapse, as though he were having a hard time staying upright. He's going to take little steps, his legs closed. If, on the contrary, this man is happy, maybe he'll have what we call a craving for life, a craving for effort, and his trunk will be, so to speak, in erection. But he won't use his arms, or his face or his hands. He has nothing to explain since he is alone. Nor any reason to smile, since he is alone.

Now, I think that we don't lie with the trunk as much as we lie with our hands. The hands and arms are distributors, dispensers, and consequently they are promisers. The face, also, is a promiser; one can lie with the face, one can lie with the arms. And if one *can* lie, there is the danger that one *is* lying.

Now, there is something else: the arms don't hold up anything whereas legs hold up the trunk. All the undertakings of the trunk and of the legs are difficult, tiring, they're demanding and they're dangerous. But the arms do a job that is not dangerous.

If Corporeal Mime were characterized, it would be with an inexpressive mask, and without arms. If arms are done away with, and if the mask does away with changes in facial expression, then there needs to be something left, and that something, that's what we're looking for.

But what is it then that happened? How did this begin? Was there only one beginning . . .?

Mime, in terms of a central concept, I didn't really invent it. It existed during the time of L'Ecole du Vieux-Colombier that Jacques Copeau directed – where, it is good to know, I was a student – a mime completely different from the old pantomime.

One day, during a diction class, the professor said to us, 'Do you know that in the other class' (he meant the more advanced class) 'they are doing interesting exercises with masks?' I said to myself, 'If their faces are covered, how could they express anything?' You can see how limited my ideas were.

So in this class, the students wore masks. But, note this well, inexpressive masks. Inexpressive, to ensure that they did not express with their faces. They wore shorts, that is to say, they were practically nude, and after a quick consultation, during which they came up with a scenario, they tried to act out short scenes on the spot. Since, what's more, they were studying ballet and gymnastics, they had in them something that was enjoyable to watch. We didn't wonder why they were naked; it was obvious that they needed to be naked, and it wasn't obscene because they were moving.

This is how I realized the importance of the mime that I called Corporeal Mime. I'm the one who gave it that name, whereas *they* used to say, strangely, 'We are working with masks.'

So why did Copeau have them do these exercises? It was to train the speaking actor. So that the speaking actor, since he is not always speaking but is present in the flesh when he isn't speaking, would master the art of moving about on the stage. The exercise was done for that reason. Its goal was not to make mime in its pure state.

Was everything already established? Was there nothing remaining but to continue? Not exactly, no, but things were far enough along for me to be taken by it. I felt right away that it was much more poetic to see people move without speaking. It was already poetry, in the sense that we already felt as if we were in another world; they moved about, and what they were doing didn't require speech. It was a charm that replaced the charm of the word, but that didn't, on the other hand, try to replace the function of the word. Obviously, they didn't look – as did the old pantomimes – as if they wished they could speak or as those people do who perform old-style pantomime, believing that they are resurrecting it whereas they are exhuming it. To these people one feels like saying, 'Well, just come on and speak, tell us what you have to say to us. Don't tire yourselves out, words were made so that we might understand each other.'

I was taken by it and I told myself that I was going to manage to do the same as they. And what was good was that they worked as much on ballet, which gave them great skill with the lower body, as they did on physical training which gave them great skill with the upper body.

But what did they do that affected me and has stayed with me?

Well, here you have it: to start with, it was the qualities of dynamic change. There were already these things that were un-dance-like. I had never seen movements in slow motion before. I had never seen prolonged immobility or explosive movements followed by a sudden petrification. This contribution to mime – these changes in the quality of the dynamics, this skill in moving one's body – that was tremendous. They taught us to appreciate immobility.

And for contrast, there was what we today call a dissolve, a slow-motion movement with an even speed, like a transported immobility, because we can have a movement that's very slow but uneven, that is more or less slow in its development. No, there it was an even slowness, it moved along like a cloud moving across the sky, when there isn't a strong wind. This also exists in mechanics, which is, let's not forget, the daughter of reason. I remember, at the train station in New York, I can still see this automobile that was turning with that even slowness on a suspended turntable. There was then this slow-motion movement that was very beautiful, and this explosion followed by immobility. These had something in common in terms of their purpose.[2]

When there is this slow-motion movement we see the trajectory through which man passes – something extraordinary! You can imagine what would happen if, at the end of our lives, we saw passing slowly before us, in thoughts, in images, everything we had done quickly. For example, we wouldn't be proud to see slowly unfolding those things we had done in anger. It seems that slowness is the condition of responsibility. Liars speak quickly, and someone who says important things, things that we can reproduce, that we can repeat, print, speaks slowly. Ah yes! The disadvantage of slowness is that it resembles immobility; it lets you see the verb 'to be'. People don't like you to see them, they are afraid that you will discover the intimacy of their person, they are afraid of being ridiculous, and this modesty, the intimacy of the verb 'to be', is greater than all the others.

Also, I liked the students' movement because it wasn't dance-like; it wasn't a half spasmodic, springing movement, a movement that seemed to happen in spite of itself. No, it was like diction, on the whole. It was a little like a thought. Sometimes this thought moves its imaginary camera through the world, and sometimes, on the contrary, it's a sudden apparition on which we fix our gaze. It was already a highly articulated way of moving. We saw what was being done; we didn't yet know what it meant, but we saw what was being done.

Did they do other things? Yes! There is something that prefigures the form I've elaborated. One day, one of our teachers did a demonstration of the art of listening, showing us how one listens in life and then how to listen in the theatre, with a translation of the head in the direction from whence the sound is coming, the head maintaining its verticality and moved by the inclination of the neck. This shook me. When I returned home, I wrote a note that is perhaps the very first thing I wrote about mime: 'The part of the body that is the first concerned is the first to act.' Since the ear was the first part concerned, and since we can't detach it from the head, that means it's the head that moves while keeping its verticality. The head doesn't do anything else; it's the neck that is at its service and then the chest and then something else. The head stays, as though it were set on a table, and as if it glides from one end of the table to the other. That's what I was able to understand.

If there hadn't been these exercises at l'Ecole du Vieux-Colombier, it's likely that I wouldn't have chosen the path I followed. What have I done? I've believed in the beauty of these exercises. I saw an artistic genre and I threw myself into it to add, to add, to add. And as I said earlier, I invented only my belief in it.

Even so, what the students did was elementary compared to what I do now. What I'm saying is not pretentious, because when one has spent a lifetime adding up little, daily discoveries, one necessarily knows more than those who began and who appealed to us at first glance.

The previous idea leads directly to segmentations of movement and to their translations. If for listening, the head makes a translation to the side as far as it can, when it reaches its limit, if you haven't yet heard, it's the chest that makes the translation of the translation of the head, and finally, if you still haven't heard, it's the legs that will translate the translation of the chest translating the translation of the head!

I felt very early on that this continuation had a moral value, a truth. The moral value is this: a thing only exists in what it continues. Everything that begins is like a verbal promise.

And it's really this that people lack: continuity. Things are easy to start; the difficulty is to continue them.

But don't take this as an infallible truth! You still must use your intelligence! The ramifications of this idea are rich and set me off on the path that has led me to the observation that the human body is like a keyboard, a keyboard that we can play, one key at a time or even several at once. I think that I contributed to this idea of a keyboard: to make one part of the body move without another. My temperament, my sense of the absolute, led me to the farthest point one can go: the bones. Not the hair, more or less curly, or the skin, but the bones. I'd like to see an X-ray film of a moving body!

There was something behind me, however, casting a light over my shoulder. I wasn't able to see the source of this light, but I walked in the light coming from this source. And this light was classical ballet. Because ballet is also a system, like mime, it's a combination of simple elements.

In the eighteenth century, the philosopher Helvétius said that to be imaginative and inventive it wasn't necessary to know lots of things, but that what was important was the combinations one makes with these things. There are people who know a lot but that doesn't make them happy; it isn't very useful to them. The mind mustn't drown in knowledge. Art only needs a few foundational principles. Look at music, what variety has been produced with only a few notes, and all this painting with only three colours.

This is certainly what my contribution to mime will have been. Inspired by the world of the Ecole du Vieux-Colombier, my path lit by the example of classical ballet and other arts, I arrived, through the mask, at Corporeal Mime, the idea that the body is a keyboard.

It was one of my students who said to me, 'The day that you said "the head without the neck", in the side inclinations, you had found your entire system.' I couldn't have found this definition, but I think it's true. That's the advantage of having students. The head without the neck, the neck without the chest, the chest without the waist, the waist without the pelvis, the pelvis without the legs, etc. . . . My innovation is to consider the human body as a keyboard. Obviously, this is an analogy, because we know very well that the human body can't function exactly like a keyboard. We can always, on a keyboard, isolate one note from another, whereas we can't isolate the chest from the head. If the chest moves, that means the head is doing something. But, nevertheless, the spirit of it is there. Nothing should be done with the body without it being intentional and calculated. Let the actor behave in regards to his body like the pianist in regards to a keyboard. And to someone who would say: 'Isn't that a little dry? What becomes of fantasy in all this business? What becomes of temperament? What becomes of genius?' I'll respond, you might say, humorously: 'Do you think music doesn't have fantasy? Do you think it doesn't have genius? And yet it also has a keyboard and alongside the keyboard it has *solfège*, things which are written.' The musician doesn't do whatever comes into his head. He can give an account of everything he did. The musician is an accountant. And yet, with this almost geometric spirit, this spirit of accounting, we get Bach, Mozart, Wagner, Saint-Saëns, Berlioz, etc. It's extraordinary to think of music's capital.

Music seems the most faithful representative of our souls. We feel as if music is never betrayed by anything, and no one can say that it is dry! That would be a joke. And yet it's the most technical art: a musician doesn't do just anything; everything is calculated. The actor, with his body, should follow the example of the instrumentalist and say: 'My body will be a keyboard, and what I'm proposing to do, will be like *solfège*, like written music.' I am asking for the theatre, for the actor, the same system as for the musical instrumentalist.

I want a theatre where the actor is the instrumentalist of his own body, and everything he does, he does as an artist and not as someone who is only exposing his personal nature.

Talent exists or it doesn't, and if it doesn't, you can't fabricate it, and if it does, all you can do is to recognize it, that's all.

And so, there you have it. I brought that. I had confidence in that. I was more concerned about making an art form, than worried about showing genius or my talent.

Acting doesn't interest me so much; I'm not so keen on people saying that I am an extraordinary mime. And yet, I was gifted, all the same. But that doesn't interest me. Geniuses pass and art remains. If God created genius, it's man who made art. It's not up to us to worry about the creation of geniuses; God will provide. But man can create art, and I prefer what man makes.

Everyone searches for what he doesn't have. As for temperament, I had too much of it. I wasn't interested in conquering, in showing my temperament more and more. First of all, I couldn't have more than I did; one can't fabricate temperament. One can, at the very most, liberate it.

What I enjoy is making others act. Do you understand? When you make others act, you have a much greater emotion than when you act yourself.

I'll return for a moment to this question of genius, of talent, of temperament, etc. We have to say that our inspiration flags while technique brings us riches, infinite suggestions. We find in following the geometric method a quantity of figures that we never would have found otherwise. I'm saying this in passing, but if we glance at architecture, which isn't a representational art, I know, but it's still amazing to think that architecture is technical, very technical. Moreover, in general, when we speak of the main art forms, the ones that we could call our masters, some will say that music is a representational art and others will say architecture is a presentational art. Architecture doesn't represent anything, it is a thing, it presents itself. Architecture doesn't represent a building; it is a building, big, popular, made for ordinary people, etc. When we think of technical concerns, of the rational concerns of the architect, these concerns didn't prevent us from making the Kremlin, the temple of Angkor, Saint Peter's in Rome, Amiens Cathedral, Reims Cathedral, Chartres Cathedral, nor from making the Parthenon and so many things with geometric, scientific demands.

And when we look at chemistry, we have a beautiful show. Chemistry boils down to a man who, looking at nature, sees that its bodies are mixed, compound. Nature is often a mixture, too often a mixture that we create according to our own wishes. So this chemist is there and says, like Prometheus: 'I don't accept the *fait accompli*. I don't accept the world as it's been given to me.' And he is going to separate the bodies and then combine them at will. He is going to change the world. The chemist is also a typical man.

Well, here's how we should proceed: study the human body, considering it like a keyboard. We detach pieces, we group them to suit ourselves, as in music, and next we study mobile geometry. We follow lines in space that *we* call designs and there again, they have a meaning. Paths followed have a meaning, apart from the breath that we might put into them. And thus we see that speed changes meaning, etc.

We see an entire art form being created, moving and clean. And I said 'clean', that's because I thought for a second of a certain reading I did about the neo-impressionist period when the painters, who were real workers, tried to produce clean colours. That's quite moving, clean colours! Ah yes, I prefer a clean art form because fleeting art like ours has to strike with clarity each time that it strikes. Our model can't be Japanese painting, we don't have the time, it passes. When poster art existed and hadn't been replaced by photographs, I once said: 'Everyone passes by posters, and mime passes by everyone.' In these two cases there is a sort of similarity. They are fleeting arts that have to strike immediately. The audience is in the theatre and doesn't move – it's the mime that comes by and has to strike the public with his actions. In the poster, which is a speaking art, it's the world that passes by and gets slapped. In both cases they're slaps, virile acts.

You have often made a point of denouncing this type of prostitution that affected, and maybe still affects, theatre. In your opinion, what should theatre be?

Theatre? It's an odd thing! It's a *maison de rendez-vous*. In French a *maison de rendez-vous* is a bordello, but a high-class bordello. That's why we say '[house] of *rendez-vous*': there are gentlemen, men of taste, who are in power and know in advance that they are going to be in contact with Mademoiselle X or Mister Y, people who are interesting and who will be able to be conscripted, mobilized, called up, selected. Business in such a place is done very well. Whereas a real bordello, a working-class bordello, we call that a *maison de tolérance*, which means that the police tolerate it and that morality disapproves of it. These two words: *maison de rendez-vous* and *maison de tolérance*, that's what theatre is. It's the *rendez-vous* of all the arts: there is the set designer, the musician, the writer, the director, the actor. You have to see to it that everyone gets along, tolerates each other. So theatre is first of all a *maison de rendez-vous* and then of *tolérance*.

But the actor, what is an actor? He's not an artist. He's a man who has certain qualities – often – and who makes us think that he is an artist. This is a mix-up made by ordinary mortals between beauty and art. And yet, we ought to make a certain distinction; and once we've done so, we will have cut many pretentious actors down to size!

That's not art! A sunset may be considered more exciting than a painting of a sunset, but, be that as it may, a sunset is not a work of art. It can happen that the sight of a horse galloping through the prairie is more moving than the sight of the best dancer in the world. But a horse galloping along is really not a work of art. You have to know what you're talking about. We can't be worthy of every compliment. The sunset cannot be worthy of the compliment of being sublime and, at the same time, of being a work of art. Y'gotta choose! You can't mix them up: art is fashioned by man and is made up of artifice. The theatre that I wish for is an artistic theatre, that is to say where one can't get up on the stage without having learned something. But I don't mean 'learned' the way you do in schools, which are places, in general, where we exalt particular temperaments. Sometimes we say we have *interesting* students, but it's not about having interesting students – it's about having students who let themselves be taught, which is already quite a different thing.[3]

There need to be schools where one studies with the geometric spirit of Pascal. I think that's what's needed but we aren't there yet!

Theatre suffers from a fundamental evil: plays are written before they are rehearsed. That's already a vice. Nobody has ever seen anything like that in the realm of the other arts. Here's an art that presumes to be about action, but that starts with writing. And when it's written, inevitably, we try to make something interesting without using anything other than what is written. I look at what I've written and I ask myself, continuously, if it's interesting. Sentences are like train carriages that follow each other. They are attached each one to the next. Is this good, or is this bad? I would say perhaps it's inevitable.

But theatre is a thing that should be 'standing'. For things to work better, the author, the writer, should be part of the troupe, always living with it and receiving the same training as the actors. It's no small thing to know which word is appropriate after an action.

If theatre ever existed in a more or less satisfactory way, it must have been during the time of the Commedia dell'arte, because they acted following a theme and not following a text. So, one can imagine the actor had artistic diction.

Today an actor's diction is almost not artistic, it is correct. And because of being correct, it becomes realistic. We can't say that we say sentences, or produce inflexions like a great draftsman might trace something on a panel. The text should be said pretty much as the author intended. As he would say: 'You're doing too much with that!' 'You're overstepping the mark.' And the mark had been set by an author, sitting, and maybe paralysed in both legs.

The dancer and the poet have to be gymnasts, and the gymnast has to be a poet. It's the combination of these two things that's usually lacking. But there you have it – that's the way things are. In other words, the play is written before it gets rehearsed. So for the actor who really understands the craft of acting thoroughly, completely, is that actor going to be able to give his all? Of course not, because his 'all' exceeds the author's. He can't do it. So, does that mean that I, for example, when you know me, does that mean that I'm afraid of betraying the theatre? I don't have enough respect for theatre to be afraid of betraying it. I don't really care. But what would shock me is the betrayal of a system. One shouldn't declare war on reason. A system should be respected because it constitutes a whole. The speaking theatre as we know it should be respected because it is a whole. It contains within itself the great principle of compensation.

And yet, the speaking actor and the Corporeal Mime have the same soul, even if they don't have the same means of expression. I'll explain: imagine a man attached to a post and condemned to be tortured. If you gag him, you won't hear his cries of pain, but you will see his movements, and if, on the other hand, you tie him up, and take off the gag, you will no longer see his movements, but you will hear his cries of pain. We could almost have these two processes repeat in alternation and you would say, 'It really is the same man and it really is the same suffering.' Sometimes we recognize the suffering through the voice and sometimes we recognize it by the movements which are intended to be seen.

So what are we going to do in theatre? What will someone who has studied mime do in the speaking theatre? I know something about this because, after all, I earned my living as a speaking actor. And remember that I started to study mime at the age of twenty-five with passion and patience, so that, if you will, ten years later I knew infinitely more about it than my colleagues. And I sure wasn't supposed to distract from the text. So, the actor can at least do something and prove his intelligence through his diction. I'm going to tell you how.

Diction is mime, vocal mime. Those inflexions that are intended for your ears are analogous to those inflexions intended for your eyes. It's mime. So there you have it, this vocal mime comes to complete the text. What will the mime that's intended for the eyes do? Above all, it wants to avoid drawing attention to itself. There is a maxim, I never figured out where it came from, that says, 'Always present and invisible'.[4] That's the commandment that you must give the speaking actor who has studied mime. His art of mime must always be present and invisible. In other words, unnoticed. And what is he going to do?

Already we see an important limitation because in the theatre nothing happens. I thank you for not having smiled, because often, when I say that, they smile, they believe that I'm being witty, sarcastic. No, it's a compliment. And it's reasonable, because there are words. Why would something material happen? Words are made in order to say the actions, and therefore spare us from having to show the actions. And there is a certain charm in one telling you the action, rather than in showing it. Because memory and imagination, on their own, already create poetry. So what does the speaking theatre devote itself to, if nothing happens in it? It's playing; it's a ballet, like a *pas de deux*, for example. I believe it would be better to call it a fist-fight between promise and threat. In the air there is a promise, a threat, we don't know how it will turn out.

When I was a student, I saw a lot of plays at the Vieux-Colombier theatre, and none of them ever excited me like the student exercises [described above] did. And yet none of that prevented me from being a speaking actor. Let me say it again: I had to earn a living. What can I say – I did what was required! Through force of circumstance, I did cinema, acting in maybe thirty-five films, in roles that were unimportant except for a few, luckily, for me. And, I might add by the way, it's funny to think that the films that weren't successful are the ones that are still shown today while the ones that were very successful are no longer shown. It's not flattering for the human race to think that today they still play *L'Affaire est dans le sac* (*It's in the Bag*, 1932), which was a total failure. And I acted in it, so I seem like a star, a retrospective star. There you have it. It's like that for everything. There aren't any exceptions. A Ravel is appreciated later. A Beethoven is appreciated later. Not right away.

I did radio and, at the same time, I said to myself: 'Perhaps it would be better if I did mime.' I had studied ballet from the age of twenty-five and that's where I had to transform it into dramatic movement. And in the area of mime, I had to count on myself. So, secretly, hiding out, in my spare time, I would do mime. Mime was my pastime, and pastime it will remain. No one will even remember that I was a speaking actor. We don't choose our profession, but we choose our pastime.

Well, mime (*laughter*), that was my pastime. Do you understand? It's mime that I loved. It's with mime that I had a love relationship, but my love for mime wasn't a lovesick kind, a caressing kind. No, it was one of struggle, as when one is fighting for one's country. It wasn't about throwing myself into the arms of something, the way we would throw ourselves into the arms of a mistress. No! It was about struggling for an obsession – all for an idea that doesn't change: the *idée fixe*. There you have something important, the obsession: to love but one thing! But how do you manage to love only one thing? It's because we see the entire world condensed in this thing. And I don't worry about it. I teach what I think it's good to teach in order to make beautiful things. Others ought to do as I do. I don't ask: 'What's this used for?' The only things in the world that are interesting are those which serve no purpose. I know a country, which I don't want to name, where, if you proposed something, the answer could be heard: 'What purpose does it serve?' And, in that same country, the younger generation has kept the expression while changing the meaning entirely, to say about wealth: 'But what is the purpose of it?' The only things that are worth loving are those that don't serve any purpose. To ask me what purpose it serves, that appals me. It seems as if we're making that question mundane. Ask me if it's beautiful, if it means something, if it can save the world if we follow the thing. I am an activist of the thing, and I need other activists. But activists are not the kind that are going to get rich. In the theatre as it is today, it's not even worth it to study anything at all, it's even better not to study anything at all. You'd get accused of being artificial. You'd get accused of not being natural. Theatre isn't an art. Is cine-matography an art? Maybe. It's a way of using bits and pieces that aren't artistic and then distributing them in a way that ends up interesting everyone. You can make a very good film without having a single artist in it.

Look, just consider the fact that in France there is a man, who is certainly not an idiot, whose name is Bresson, a director who demands actors he hires – they aren't even actors – to have never studied anything at all. I even have a buddy who tried out for a role with Bresson saying that he had never studied. So Bresson said to him: 'Read me this article in *France-Soir*.' He read it. Bresson listened and then said to him: 'I can tell that you have studied.' He responded, 'Yes, I admit it.' 'Get out of here, sir!' He left.

So there is a very good film director, a very good composer of films, who insists that the person he's going to use should never study anything. You're going to say to me: 'That's an exception. You shouldn't generalize.' Yes, there are exceptions that didn't exist, [and] that exist and that we want to gen-eralize from. If I had the beginnings of tuberculosis, that would be an exception. But it would still be better to go for treatment early enough on! Do you think you could put a man who has never studied an instrument into an orchestra? Can we conceive of that, even as an exception? Of course not! Because music is an art and film isn't. Perhaps it is one, if you like, but not where the actor is concerned. When you have an actor with a crooked spine and you want to make him straight, they'll say to you: 'But you're going to deform him!' I saw an actor like that, who arrived in New York from Hollywood, a tall young man, very nice, at that, who was earning a good living in Hollywood. He was precious: they needed a man with a twisted spine, and it was he. So here I was trying to make him straight, because he came to take lessons at our studio. He said to his friends: 'He's working hard to make me straight.' So they said to him: 'He's going to deform you!' That's what the film industry is like.

No, honestly, I think that theatre is not an art. It's a *rendez-vous* of arts where the main ingredient is missing: the actor. If the poor guy has studied anything at all, they'll criticize him. You see, I feel as if studying mime is a very good way to get turned down wherever you try to get in. That's what mime is good for. Not only is it of no useful purpose, it's good for getting all the doors closed to you. We have to dedicate ourselves to mime the way the first Christians dedicated themselves to Christianity. Like the first socialists dedicated themselves to socialism. It's activists that we need. And the question – 'What is it good for?' – doesn't interest me, it appals me.

It's mime that interested me, the mime of the body.

And why the mime of the body? Because it's the body that pays the bill, that suffers, that wants, that proves, and when I see a body rise up, it's humanity itself rising up.

At the heart of it, I find that there are political arts and others that are more religious. We sense that on one side we have Jesus Christ and on the other Prometheus. If we take painting, for example, it leans readily towards religion, dance also, singing, not always, but readily, whereas rhyming poetry is already approaching reason and it's already a little bit Promethean. If we take sculpture, it's Promethean, and if we take mime in the way that I understand it, it's Promethean and I contrast it to dance in that sense.

There you have it, I don't really know what this talk is worth. It's maybe not even a talk but a chat. There was no plan followed, but these are, nonetheless, lively ideas.

So, always, my spare time was filled with mime. And one day, I prepared a short piece. I did a lot of things all by myself. I had to, because the students I trained would leave, one after another. One day I said: 'Now I am going to do my piece all by myself.' That's what was beneficial for me. That allowed me to go here and there to show what I was doing, things I wanted to do and wanted to develop. That's how things . . . and so it happened that little by little I wound up making a name for myself . . . A type of retrospective propaganda was happening already, it was already starting. And my school opened officially in 1942, those 'gentlemen' [the Nazis] were still there. The school developed like that, little by little.

The first piece I made was *Primitive Life*.

I didn't know how to swim, and I started right away by depicting swimming. I opened a dictionary and I looked up the word *swimming*. There were pictures that showed the different strokes. There was breaststroke, backstroke, sidestroke, crawl, all sorts of strokes like that. I said to myself: 'I'm going to do it.' There were dives into the water: 'I will dive onto the floor', and obviously at the same time there was the boat. Being in the boat, you had to row, you had to fall out of the boat, you had to climb back in the boat. A whole story around water which was even funnier in that I didn't know how to swim.

What else happened? What difficulties did I encounter?

I'm going to tell you about one – it was very, very difficult. It was even dangerous. In acrobatics there is a thing that acrobats call *la courbette*, maybe because the body manages to make a curve [*une courbe*]. I'm going to tell you what that consists of: you get set, the idea is to jump, in other words to jump off your feet and to land on your hands in exactly the same place as where your feet were. It's very difficult. So I did a *courbette* that I followed with a forward roll and I got up after this forward roll. So it looked as if I had dived into the water and wound up doing the breaststroke. I would fall out of the boat while making these movements. Then I had to climb back into the boat. And my wife was in the boat – that was a whole other story. So there you have swimming! And there were so many other things!

But, from the swimming, you had to think about fish. You had to think about the net that you throw. How do you throw one so that it's well done and where do you throw it from? You throw it from the boat and then after the net, filled with fish, we pull the net, we pull, pull, we carry it to the beach. And so there you have the fish jumping out of the net. We try to catch them, but they slip out of your hand. And on and on! And all of that . . .

But since we were outside, it occurred to us, of course, to climb to the top of a tree to pick fruit. Little by little we knew that our work would be called *Primitive Life*. That is to say, people who live from fishing, hunting and picking fruit. So that's the direction we went in. We had to climb to the top of the tree and then climb back down. It was a whole thing, going from branch to branch, for it to seem real. Passing fruit to each other, and we had to eat it; and since we had masks, we had to move the head in a way that would make people think that we were chewing, that we were biting into the fruit, whereas in reality they couldn't see our mouths. So there you have it! So, after we had done that, I thought of something I could have thought of earlier, which was counterweights.

But before I speak of that, I have to tell you something else. I met Jean-Louis Barrault, a brand new student at Dullin's, who wanted to participate in our piece *Primitive Life*. So I said to him: 'Listen, it's not so easy, I performed this piece in public with my wife, it's ready to go. I'd be happy to have you in it, but I don't know what I'm going to do.' So he said to me: 'I'll play another character who watches you.' – 'Ah, that's a very good idea.' And indeed, that suited him well, and he became the man who wanted to make love with my wife and who considered me an enemy. Then there was a whole little drama, and we found ourselves face to face, each trying to grow taller than the other, as if we were trying to grow a few inches taller by stretching upwards. And at that point, each of us grabbed something that looked like a lance and the combat started. That's how *Ancient Combat* was born, which obviously would require very fast counterweights. But Barrault was very talented, and so was I, for this kind of counterweight. So that's what we did.

When I started studying mime, I was immediately captivated by the depiction of material things. Right away I sensed that if speaking theatre can speak of things that occurred elsewhere – that's what words are for – mime necessarily needs to show things.

And what then are those things? They're necessarily material things. Before the memory of something, which is a spiritual thing, there has to be the thing itself that we remember. Right away I was attracted to these activities: swimming, climbing to the top of a tree, fighting. So, my first activity was *Primitive Life*. I wanted to go from this primitive life to a craftsman's life and it seemed to me a good idea to choose *The Carpenter*. I don't think I was influenced by Jean-Jacques

Rousseau, because I hadn't yet read *Emile*, where he decides, after much thought, to choose for his spiritual son the carpenter's profession. A carpenter is a man who thinks: he calculates; he's a geometrician and an artist. He has to make a form, which is a creation. Geometry and art: it's really extraordinary to think that this relatively modest trade assumes that one can have the abilities of a geometrician, an exact science, and the abilities of an artist.

And as though that weren't enough, that man, setting him as we did in the distant past, had to be able to fell a tree. So, Barrault and I looked for a tree in the forest. He had to cut it down, move it before sawing it lengthwise into long thick sections, and in order to move it he had to be on horseback. And how could he be on horseback? So the two of us played the horse. Barrault was at the back, he was the horseman, and at the same time, with his buttocks, he made the buttocks of the horse. As for me, I was in front, with my body, my trunk, I represented the horse's neck, with my head, the horse's head, and my legs were the horse's front legs. And the two of us headed off like that. It looked like a horse, we were told. And Barrault, I might add, later worked on the horse all by himself – he had fallen in love with that horse. Next he had to get off the horse, he had to cut down the tree, he had to be the lumberjack. It was a whole thing!

Once the tree was moved, he had to chop it into pieces. Don't forget that the word *menuisier* [carpenter, in French] means to 'make small'.

One wonders, when you think about it a bit, what *doesn't* the carpenter do? He does everything, for all intents and purposes. If we look at it from the point of view of the drama, we see that he hesitates, that he concentrates, that he thinks. At certain moments, on the other hand, everything's fine. It's all about putting a lot of energy into it, to work with rhythm, the way one does when scrubbing a floor, when, for example, he's planing the wood. So, precision, meticulousness, heavy work: he's an accomplished man. It makes you wonder if there could be any area in which he would be lacking. It's the flowering of all human faculties, and as Jean-Jacques Rousseau observed, it's an honest profession.

The carpenter has contact with wood, which is a beautiful material, a pleasant material, almost alive. The carpenter is a man who still knows botany a little. He has to choose from among the trees; the trees have their specificities. When it's a question of building furniture, some of them – like the ash tree – are a little too flexible. He also has to know how the wood should be treated, because he is going to need to let it dry a long time and it's going to buckle. What a to-do! The carpenter's world is really something! Having seen how widespread this activity is, how dramatic it is, because it's made up of all the moral phenomena – hesitation, trust, retrospective examination: has he made a mistake or not? Should he risk it? – we are necessarily inclined to think that it's a beautiful subject.

But little by little it occurs to us that it's like the reflection, or rather the prefiguration, of abstract mime. Indeed, when man thinks, he struggles with ideas the way we struggle with matter. Since we don't see ideas, since we don't see thought, since we don't have a direct hold on thought, the best thing is to do a material job that requires intelligence and where the gestures are like the echo of our intelligence.

With regards to the technique that's in *The Carpenter*, that takes a long time to explain. To explain technique with words is no small task. I can at least give the general ideas. Here's one: the point was to depict *The Carpenter*. That's a generality. A generality is not an abstraction, we know, but it resembles an abstraction all the same. When we say 'liberty' or 'intelligence' it's in our mind, they are abstractions. While we're out for a walk, we're in no danger of colliding with intelligence and getting a bump on the forehead. Nor have we ever seen *the* horse walking in the street: that's a generality. We've encountered *a* horse, but not *the* horse. We've never seen *the* Frenchman, we've seen *a* Frenchman. And it's like that with everything. *The* Carpenter, we've never seen him either.

Were we supposed to depict a carpenter, a man of fifty-five, with a cigarette butt hanging out of his mouth? Should he have a cap, or should he be bare-headed? Should he be strong, fat or thin? All these questions. The best thing was for the actor to be in trunks, without clothes or costume. This idea of generality, we find in the acting itself. It's not about dealing with particular cases, but always with generalities. What more could you do, when you can't show movements at the same time as speaking? Mime isn't allowed to use speech – speech which is a marvellous thing; speech, which is the glory of humanity and so many other things – [isn't allowed to use] this mountain of poetry that speech produces. So he has to invent another kind of speech. And, precisely, he has to strive to make us feel what happens when we think everything has stopped: resonance.

Imagine a man who is in a world where everyone is deaf, but sees clearly, and this man beats on a gong. As soon as he hits the gong, all the deaf people think that the action is over, that the act of hitting the gong doesn't have any consequences. But if there are some people next to them who are not deaf, but blind, for them, everything begins after the clang of the mallet on the gong, when the resonance starts. Maybe we are deaf to many things ourselves. There are things that we throw into space and that stop even though they should continue. There are things that need to resonate and mime very often allows them to. We have to imagine that we have audience members who are deaf: they see the thing that starts but they don't see the continuation. We have to extract from the world – where things are hidden – the things that are hidden within things.

In *The Carpenter*, in particular, he makes certain gestures with a certain strenuous effort, and, as it would do in water, this gesture wants to continue. In practical, everyday life, this gesture is stopped. It's as if actions are like hair, they want to grow, but social life, or even other necessities, make you cut your hair very short. So that we don't understand the whole truth, the full potential of things. We see what they are, but not what they want to be. So, in *The Carpenter*, lots of movements are the continuation of something that usually gets cut by the social scissors.

After making *Primitive Life* and *Artisanal Life*, I found myself completely alone to do *The Factory*. So that little by little I called my activity: *The Three Ages*. That is to say, to speak like an economic historian, the three ages of production: primitive life, then when the instrument was found, artisanal life, and then it's on to the machine.

All of this was performed with our bodies, could be performed with our bodies, and we made spectacular things that were enjoyable to watch, and it involved only material things. So of course they said: 'You only deal with material things!' Good grief, how people dislike matter! They always want to show their souls. Watch out for people who want to show you their souls! Are they really worth being exposed? I say this ironically, but it's often the case. Someone who doesn't have a soul often wants to show it. And one can always pretend that one is expressing his soul by doing whatever. But you can't make people believe that you're playing a carpenter, washing clothes or swimming by doing any old thing. You have to work, discipline yourself. And people don't like work: they want to ascend to the throne while climbing down. That's why they like skiing, by the way, it's because it's downhill. Their punishment is that they often break a leg. When I see an intellectual show up with a broken leg because he was skiing, that makes me smile a little; I say to myself, that's his punishment. If he climbed a mountain, I would have pity for him, but in skiing, he was going downhill. Ah! They like skiing; they feel as if they're rising up to the heavens while coming down. They have the law of gravity at their service. But I'm getting a little off the subject.

There were other reasons: the fact is that very often man expresses his feelings through words. But when he makes something, it's not his words that make it. And it wasn't bad that this mime, not satisfied with being an alternate expression for words, should try, if possible, to express something else. [Mime expresses] a whole world that would have been neglected, a touching world, a world which deserved to be told about. If you travel, if you visit a factory, you see things. If you watch a fire, you watch the firemen, you see what they do. With sports, you see things. And we feel as if we go back to our common mother, into the human womb, into the origin of the world, because at the beginning of the world, we had to do *something*. We had no choice but to tackle matter.

And tackling matter is dramatic. Matter does not let itself be worked so easily; there are obstacles. There are animals too, which maybe are not made of inanimate material, but anyway they are not things that we *tell*, they are things that we *encounter*, and that's the difference. Describing a bear in words is not the same thing as having one in front of you. But there was another reason, and that is that in a speaking play we speak of things and what we speak of are often material things. We say of a man, 'He does such and such a job.' We've just referred to a materiality. We say: 'He did such and such a thing, he did a material thing.' But since we said it, we don't need to show it. And that's precisely the charm of spoken theatre, the fact that it doesn't show a lot. When it does show something, which is the case for example with a duel, as we have in *Hamlet*, as we have in Corneille's *Le Cid*, or an action like a murder, in *Othello*, it doesn't work so well. It feels as if the spoken play stops in order to show us a music hall number. Yes, and so mime can stop the action of a spoken play. It's striking, the action that distracts us from the action. It's almost a contradiction in terms. Well, *we* [mimes] act too, we depict active things that remind us of the human condition, the fundamental condition. But since we can't tell about it, since we don't work, we have no other choice but to show these actions.

And so that's why the mime artist needs to know how to make material things; and that doesn't prevent him from making spiritual things especially since he can put spiritual things in his work, in the representation of a material thing. You're going to say that I'm repeating myself, but what does it matter; if you take, for example, *The Carpenter*, it's abstract mime in a certain sense, and if it isn't, it's just as good as abstract mime, in that man is obliged to think before acting. We have a clear sense, when he tackles the wood, that he mustn't destroy the wood. He has to give it the desired form and not an undesired form. He mustn't damage the material, nor waste it, as it's expensive. He mustn't injure himself either: because if he injures himself, his work is disrupted. So he has to make calculations as he works; he hesitates, he makes up his mind, and suddenly he goes at it. It's a great deal of work, he does it, and all of a sudden he stops and wonders: 'Did I make a mistake? Is it good? And what do I have to do now?' He checks it, he brushes his hand across it to see if it's really flat, he corrects it, and we see that this man hasn't stopped thinking and that all the ways of thinking within this thought were experienced by him: hesitation, doubt, decision, continuous will, perseverance, review, a long look over things. He did everything, everything that you can describe in psychology, he did it, he performed it. What music also does quite well, in this area, he did. And then afterwards, he tackles feelings, and he really needs to know how to express feelings that don't apply to a material action. And so he does that, and there is a whole other poetry in that.

There you have it!

That's how this got started! I started studying mime as a student in 1925. Then I gave my first public shows in 1930 and 1931. And yet, before appearing before the general public, I performed first for two or three people, sometimes there were even five! And I noted carefully everything these people told me. I haven't lost those notes. It's funny when you reread what you've written! My biggest regret is that I don't have much time left to carry out all the projects that I want to. I don't see mime's end. I consider what I have done to be meagre when I think of what could be done. And I'll say it again: I didn't invent anything – I only invented believing in it!

I also didn't invent anything because I'm hostile towards novelty.

I don't like novelty. When someone proposes something new, it's because he's too lazy to extract the best out of something old.

I remember a lecture that Jacques Copeau gave in London in 1924. He said these words that seem quite reactionary: 'He who turns towards the future, it's because he lacks the will to turn towards the past.' The future is a chain of ideas, the past is a chain of completed acts.

Looking to the past, seeing the works that remain, keeps us from being pretentious.

That makes me think of a passage in one of [Jean] Jaurès's speeches: 'We are accused of not loving the past!' And addressing [politicians on] the Right, he said: 'We love the past, we have kept its flame; you have kept only the ashes.'

I have tried to make myself a defender of these words and it hasn't been very hard for me to do!

How can one be a revolutionary politically and not artistically? I have been a partisan of socialism since I was eleven, and consequently a partisan of political revolution, and I've almost always, by my nature, been conservative in art. So one could say that's surprising. There is another surprising thing: to see political reactionaries who are avant-garde in art. I've known plenty of them. I've asked myself if my father wasn't right when he would say: 'Artists are monarchists, because it's only to the rich that they can sell their paintings.' I can still see myself with a man who was a supporter of abstract painting and who wouldn't allow a machine to scrub the floor. He felt that women should scrub the floors themselves. I've known others, a host of others, and it's easy to explain why. Man gets bored and wants things to be shaken up a bit, so when one is conservative in politics, there have to be other things that move. So one feels as though one is engaging in revolutionary activity in reading Stéphane Mallarmé. We move ideas about, we turn things upside down, but the safe [the strongbox] is always in its place. So don't be astonished that I, who am subversive in the political sphere, would be conservative in art.

Mime doesn't move ideas about and doesn't create new ones: it makes the old ideas new. It's like a country priest, it doesn't need to be avant-garde.

I don't believe that mime's special function is to depict capitalism as being better than socialism, and that the best way to achieve socialism is to follow Bakunin's method, or, on the contrary, to follow the Marxist method with the thesis, the antithesis or the *foutaise*.[5] No, all of that doesn't interest me. Obviously I am for Trotsky when he is driven out by Stalin. But if Trotsky were in power, I would be against him. No, it's not that, I'm speaking of political breath, of Promethean breath. When a man is stretched out on the ground, in briefs, in shorts, it's very simple, it's a people that are lying down and then you see them slowly rising up. You see the whole muscular play in his movement, and then he comes, he goes, he lifts things up, he hurls them. It's man relying on himself and that's the sense in which it's a Promethean art. It's exemplary, this mime, it makes one want to do likewise, it gives one the desire to lift oneself up. It's like Victor Hugo. When one reads Victor Hugo, one says to oneself, you can't just remain where you are. You have to do something.

And mime should above all, above all, want to say to men – because it's the muscle that acts – 'Everything is possible.' It's the will that's lacking, it's not the power. Mime is the art form that should be exemplary. It is almost condemned to be exemplary. And why 'condemned'? Because we can't allow ourselves, when we are in shorts on the stage, to be limp. A nude, on stage, must always be in action. A little like athletes: they should always be in action. There you have some observations that I could speak about for three days, but one has to know how to restrain oneself. What is most lacking in men, when one thinks about it, is the will, it's a steadfast will. Man works to earn a living, and when he has finished his day, he doesn't feel like taking on the higher interests of humanity. He feels like sleeping, so he behaves like a lazy person, with regard to the nation. And that's the way he is. We let catastrophes come, we let them ripen. They don't come because people want them to, they come because people want to sleep. 'We can't do anything about it, if it has to happen, it's better not to know!' Humanity has always been faced with the greatest of threats, these threats aren't decreasing, but there you have it. . . . 'One has to sleep.' Sleep! But, here's what I say, we can't do mime while sleeping.

Could you speak to us about Jacques Copeau, Charles Dullin, Louis Jouvet, Antonin Artaud, all these people who influenced you and with whom you worked?

Obviously it's not very modest to say this, but I have not been subject to influences. Aside from the Vieux-Colombier, with its exercises, I have not been subject to any influence. But, on the other hand, I have received consolation. It's not much fun, you know, to be all alone in thinking something, so consolation is very important.

91

At the Vieux-Colombier, there was the school on the one hand and the theatre on the other – students on the one hand, and actors on the other. That's what you have to keep in mind: when I praise the Vieux-Colombier, I am mostly praising the school. Which is not to say that the Vieux-Colombier theatre was of no interest, on the contrary! But it's the school that interested me. What did one do in this school? They tried to give the student a real humanity. The students received an education whose aim was to develop, or at least broaden, their humanity. They taught them Greek philosophy, Greek religion, so that they'd understand Greek theatre better. From there, they went on to the theatre of the Middle Ages, they got to the Commedia dell'arte and they exposed them to the theatre of the seventeenth century, etc., etc. – a big overview of the theatre, without forgetting, of course, the Orient. There was a course on the Japanese Noh that was quite carefully prepared. There was also a course, given by a specialist, about costume: costumes through the ages, and the students were taught how to make their own costumes. There was a sculpture class, taught by a sculptor, and there, too, the students made their own masks. In fact, they became sculptors each in his or her own way. They were taught the history of music. And so many other things! There were, for all intents and purposes, as many teachers as students!

Twice a week we went to the circus to work under the direction of the Fratellini brothers. I fell in love with the circus world. I went there often. I was allowed to go backstage and I would go up on the bleachers. It was exhilarating. One can't be a circus star without proving oneself worthy of being a circus star. There was another thing that I noticed in circus people: modesty. There was a circus puritanism! As for me, I ran into trouble because I wore . . . I wore something like shorts, you know. I had on briefs. I did what I could, you know, to keep people from seeing a certain protuberance. But it wasn't enough. Even in the rehearsals, it wasn't enough. So, there was Paolo who went and got one of my friends and said to him:

'You have to tell your friend, okay? . . . He should do whatever it takes, okay? . . . Because we can still see, we see . . .'

They didn't even say what they saw. So I bought underwear.

'So, what's the story? Your friend still hasn't done anything?'

'Oh yes he *has!* He bought a new pair of underwear.'

'He doesn't buy the right underwear. You need to speak with him.'

It was serious. This puritanism is extraordinary.

But let's get back to the Vieux-Colombier! As for the students, they had good living conditions. So that they wouldn't be distracted, or running all over the place, to rush through school and start acting right away, they were subsidized. They received a little stipend that permitted them to live. There were around ten of them, at most. It was quite serious. On the other side, there was the theatre, in other words, the stage with the actors.

What did Copeau do in all this? He necessarily took care of the theatre in general, and then financial and administrative questions. Enough worries to keep one from sleeping at night! But he was obviously, and above all, a director. He was an actor also. He had a wonderful voice, amazing articulation that had a kind of incisiveness that didn't seem forced. He was a good actor ... who perhaps could have used a director (*laughter*). Sometimes he would have acted better if he had had a director guiding him. He wasn't a man whose background was in the theatre; instead he came to this having had a literary background.

Copeau would have liked his actors to know how to move and [would have liked them] to move. But how do you make actors move when they haven't yet learned the science of bodily movement? What do you do?

Copeau seems to me, through his school, to have been the innovator. Without the work that was done at that school, I wouldn't have got the idea of the 'thing'.

I still remember when Jacques Copeau said to me: 'You ought to have a kind of mime that's like the movements that I do with my arms when I do a reading.' He thought that, in this way, one would be moving away from the mime that consisted of imitating material things.

Dullin had the same tendency that Copeau did – this taste for movement – but with actors that hadn't been trained for that. They were younger; it seemed as if we were members of a student theatre. But, don't get me wrong, I mean it in the best sense of the term!

Dullin was as in love with poetic verse as I am. Obviously, he mostly read mournful poems: Verlaine, Baudelaire, Villon and others. He would recite them with extraordinary talent. I like these poets too – I like everything that is beautiful. However, there was a difference between the two of us: I was a supporter of health, and Dullin had a certain affinity for malady. But each of us liked poetry as much as the other.

I remember one rehearsal. I can still see the author, a remarkable woman who had written a Breton[6] play. It was a very masculine play (she herself was very masculine), but what she wrote was really beautiful. I was starting out as a prompter, stage manager, I was supposed to note what should be cut. I helped with everything, I was there from start to finish. And here was Dullin, this man who loved poetry so much, who recited it so well, who asked that we cut a big part of it. And I can still see the woman saying: 'You're cutting that? Really Monsieur Dullin, one can't write a play in telegraphic style.' Dullin wanted to cut everything that was poetic. He responded: 'Yes. Yes. But it stops the action.' And it was true; it stopped the action. A play is like a river that, instead of running down from the mountain, climbs *up* the mountain. It mustn't stop; there mustn't be time for the audience to think. The audience is like an aeroplane that no longer has an engine, and that is being pulled by another aeroplane. If the aeroplane that's pulling goes slowly, the one that is being pulled hangs off of it with too much slack. And the audience is similar, you have to pull it without stopping . . . If you stop, the audience realizes that they are at the theatre. And then, you have to bring them back up, start them up all over again. That requires something of a rhythm; you can't have stops that are too long.

Dullin adored spontaneity. He liked what we call the impulsive. He was hungry for authenticity, he always watched us with a lot of interest, as if he were at a fishing expedition. He would wait for the moment where something would spring up. He was an extremely nice man. We had great trust and great respect for him. And he didn't need to be firm to gain respect. We liked him without trying to, just as he was, with his tantrums. We liked him. I even feel as if we liked him more than we liked Copeau. I liked Dullin more than Copeau, but I considered myself Copeau's student, I didn't feel like Dullin's student. But Dullin was extremely refined; his stage direction was always extremely interesting. If I don't speak of him in my book *Words on Mime*, it's because he didn't teach me anything in terms of mime.

When Dullin saw my first attempts [at mime], which were done independently of him, as it were, he was filled with enthusiasm. He wasn't jealous; it didn't bother him to see that I could do something different. For him it was something other than what he was working on, but he looked on it favourably. He even offered to have me perform on his stage, at least for a private audience, my first important production done with Jean-Louis Barrault. He even offered me his favourite composer, Marcel Delannoy, who was part of the *Groupe des six* that was spoken of so much during that period, so that he would compose music for us. But I didn't want music.

Dullin always looked on my work favourably.

As for Antonin Artaud, he didn't teach me anything, but I appreciated what he was doing. We understood each other, and we understood each other without speaking – there was a kind of mutual affinity there. He looked on me as a man who wasn't like the others and I looked on him as a man who wasn't like the others. A woman who had been his mistress – very beautiful by the way – said to me one day: 'You remind me of Antonin Artaud.'

He had me act in two plays – they weren't his plays, but Strindberg's, whom he quite liked; so he chose me, he didn't take just anyone. He chose those who had a different way of acting. Another time, I was in several of his productions, one of which was a play by him. I remember that there were only surrealist plays. And in that one too, I could see what he wanted, I sensed a kind of kinship between us. I quite liked what he did in speaking theatre. We had a point in common, which was the fact that we were anti-realist.

We were really like two brothers, but we were never able to speak at great length.

Let's talk about Jouvet now. He didn't really have a school. In all theatres there is always some bit of school, but it doesn't always deserve that name. With Jouvet instead of saying that there was a school on one side and a theatre on the other, we could say that there was Jouvet on one side and the other actors on the other. And yet Jouvet willingly surrounded himself with actors who were as important as he, people of great ability. We saw people like Valentine Tessier, who was a star; we saw Pierre Renoir, the son of the great painter, who was a real star, who was known to everyone.

There was something in Jouvet's instinct, in his temperament, that I liked. One could sense in him a taste for the marionette – a way of turning the head, of using his neck, of standing a certain way. One already felt the articulated man. It didn't go much further than that, but he had that in his blood.

Ideologically, Jouvet's acting appealed to me. I was enlightened by the school of the Vieux-Colombier. With Dullin it was something else. It was Dullin who trained me, who fixed me. He took me on in an utterly rudimentary state. He showed me what it was to give my all and kept me from going overboard. He tried to give me what they call 'good taste': a taste for moderation while still keeping the passion. I was impassioned during my time with him! His acting filled me with enthusiasm. But that doesn't mean that it took on a doctrinal character. If we look at it from a doctrinal point of view, the idea comes from the school of the Vieux-Colombier, with Copeau, and style came to me from Jouvet. But all of that in a rudimentary state, of course.

I would be an imbecile, if, after spending so many decades working, I hadn't taken it further.

I have seen many things, and I've seen so much that it leads me, when we do something with mime, to say, 'But you know, the thing I just told you about, that can be found in the street. All you have to do is walk down the street to see what I've just explained to you.' Often I say, 'I'm not inventing anything, not in technique, not in poetry, not in symbolism.'

So if I'm not inventing anything, what am I doing? What is my worth? I move stuff! I'm not an inventor, I am a 'furniture mover'. Which means that I go here and there and that there are things that come into me, principles that penetrate me. I take a principle from somewhere or other and I apply it to the theatre, which doesn't have its own principles. I think we don't invent anything. What we take for an invention is a relocating. We take a principle that is applied somewhere, and we move it. There is an obligatory principle of rhythm in versification. So we take it, we move it and we put it in movement of the body. It's not an invention – obviously, we invent its relocation . . . yes, maybe this relocation is an invention.

Without our knowing it, maybe, in the history of man, many things that have passed for inventions are nothing but relocations.

So sometimes, when I have the feeling that I'm creating something, I correct myself and say: 'I didn't create anything; this is something that's on the street.' There is poetry on the street. There is poetry in a bar, in a restaurant. There is work everywhere, methods are used everywhere. That's what I call finding out about things without being a scholar, because I only collect what can be used for our art. Except there is something else: what I just said, I regret already, because one might imagine that I think there is only one thing in the world and that that thing is mime. Mime wouldn't interest me if I didn't feel the world vibrating when I do it.

Above all that, there is the political sense. Political sense is what is most missing in people – that true political sense which is the concern for justice and happiness, and not adherence to a political party.

We already know that philosophers speak about religious sense and that they differentiate between religious sense and adherence to a religion. One could safely say that religious sense preceded religions – that it's religious sense that gave birth to religions. When we think about it, we also say that it's atheists who have the most highly developed religious sense. How can one live without religion? I mean without a certain mystery. Why come and go, why sacrifice oneself, why work if there isn't something? And what is this something?

I will start with an image. There are two ways to receive light. You can take it in through the eyes and say, 'I am illuminated.' But you can also receive it from behind which means that you can't see a light source in front of you. We see clearly. Clear though our sight may be, it is made possible by the light source that we can't see. There are moments when you wonder whether political sense doesn't resemble religious sense.

Can you clarify for us what political sense is for you?

Careful! I'm not speaking about political parties. Many crimes have been committed because of the idea of a party. Sometimes you get the feeling that people who wanted to hurt humanity, hurt it less than those who wanted to do good for humanity in the name of a party. I don't accept injustices for the sake of a party that supposedly serves humanity.

So, what is a political sense?

We already know that *polis*, in Greek – is there anything that doesn't come to us from the Greeks? – means 'city'. Now then, for this small population, what they called the city is what we today would call humanity. Humanity! The two things that concern humanity: first justice and then happiness. And always, at every moment, when one brings up a principle of mime, one notices that it applies to 'politics'. One is speaking of justice, of happiness, of despair, of the futility of striving, the value of striving . . . Contradiction? If there weren't this contradiction, humanity would have died out a long time ago. There is fatalism, there is free will – both exist; they are in conflict. So, I was first a citizen and the arts didn't interest me. I thought that the arts didn't interest me and then one day I was sentenced to practise an art, and it happened, by chance, that it was the art of theatre.

We can't live without lunacy, without believing in something impossible. It's absolutely essential. If we saw things as they are, we would kill ourselves before too long. We have to believe in something, and when we don't believe in God, which is my case, when one doesn't have a declared religion, also my case, we give ourselves over to political lyricism – in other words, to the dream of a just and happy humanity.

But does humanity also have to be likeable? How do we like something that isn't likeable? We would like a humanity that is happy but also just. Do we want it to be happy first and then just, or do we want it first to be just and then happy? Does happiness prompt us to worry about justice on earth or does it distance us from that concern? And does the love of justice lead us to happiness? These are the questions. Regardless, whether we are mistaken or not, we dream of a happy and just humanity, and one whose happiness is not based on the misfortune of others.

Even when we protest, even when we say that we feel hopeless, political lyricism is hovering above us. And what is it? It's the love for humanity – humanity which is perhaps an abstraction.

And this reminds me of a passage from a Dostoyevsky book, *The Brothers Karamazov*, that says: 'Christians want to raise the earth up to heaven and socialists want to bring heaven down to earth.' That's awe-inspiring! You could say that from the point of view of the heart, it's the same thing. Whether you want to raise the earth up to heaven, in other words, to paradise, or if one wants to bring paradise down to earth, it's the same concern.

This same Dostoyevsky writes further on, 'the more one loves humanity, the more one hates men'. Obviously that surprises us. But it's necessary; it couldn't be otherwise. The very fact that we dream of happiness and justice means that happiness and justice don't exist. If they existed, we wouldn't dream of them, we wouldn't struggle to achieve them and we see – since one has to speak to men; one can't speak to an abstraction, the abstraction doesn't have ears, we serve it, that's all – so you have no other choice but to speak to *men*. And we discover that men don't like mankind and if men like mankind in particular, assuming that such a situation exists, we mustn't confuse men liking some men, with men who like mankind – who are concerned about far-off and invisible men.

When we speak extemporaneously, we don't say every-thing we would like to say; we sometimes forget important things. We even fall into parenthetical remarks by associating related ideas. But all in all, it's less boring because one sees the

man searching for his ideas, who might not be able to find them, and consequently it's a bit of an adventure.

And here I can't help but compare Baudelaire and Victor Hugo. Baudelaire had political concerns and he wrote a page in prose – as if by accident, it was in prose – where he says: 'Everything is bloody ruined! All is lost!' He speaks of decadence, he describes his period as though it were the one we are living at the moment, because poets are always prophets; they don't need statistics to see what's going to happen.

Hugo, in one of his poems, also says: 'All is lost!' What a difference there is between Hugo who says: 'All is lost!' and Baudelaire who says, 'All is lost!' It's that one feels that Baudelaire, in the depth of his soul, truly thinks that all is lost whereas in Hugo, one feels that he's insulting the people by saying to them: 'Everything is bloody ruined!' But it's to slap them, to strike them on their cheek, to wake them up. He still hopes – one feels it by his anger. He isn't hopeless, because he's shouting abuse, insults. One is not hopeless when one insults, whereas in Baudelaire, one feels that all is lost.

I've sometimes said that Baudelaire is the sick brother of Victor Hugo.

Goethe said this sentence which I find unforgettable: 'Humanity only needs masterpieces.' The sentence, as it is constructed, tempts me and I would say, 'Humanity only needs optimists.' Humanity doesn't need pessimistic prophets, pessimistic poets, it needs optimistic prophets. Corneille is an optimist and Hugo is an optimist and I am an optimist.

Because, when I say, 'All is lost!' the very fact that I say it proves that all is not lost. Why say, 'All is lost!' if all is not lost?

It's that we hope for something, we hope to awaken indifferent people. This I owe to my father – [a sense of] justice and injustice.

It goes without saying that justice is above beauty, even though we don't really know what beauty there could be that wouldn't bear the mark of justice. I'm certainly not going to allow the massacre of civilians because I'm busy with painting. If they said to me, 'You know, you could stop this massacre, we're counting on you,' my answering, 'Ah, I can't, I'm busy, because I have a client, I'm going to make a painting that depicts the massacre. But believe me, my thoughts are with you. I feel this massacre so strongly that I'm going to make a fantastic work about this massacre,' – that would be pathetic.

And now look at yourselves. You will see that you can live without Art, but you can't live without justice. Hours pass in which we live without Art. There aren't that many people who read poetry. There aren't that many people who enjoy being in a museum; some go to be bored collectively, and so on. They go to the theatre to talk about it during intermission. So imagine that you are in a museum, suppose that you are a painter and that you see a painting that you can't stand. And you say: 'They shouldn't have hung such a thing.' The ugliness of this painting is not going to keep you from sleeping, it won't spoil your appetite, it won't make you sad. It allows you to make conversation, to say, at the table, 'I saw an atrocious, dreadful, abject, disgusting, vomit-inspiring, you know, horrible, atrocious, terrible painting, my dear lady. Ah! But it was – let's say the word – revolting.' It allows you to say all that. And people would say to each other: 'There's a man who has taste.'

If, on the other hand, you, as painter, have a committee refuse your painting for an exhibition, saying that it wasn't good, whereas without being arrogant, you are convinced that your painting deserves to be shown, you feel as if you're the victim of an injustice and you'll think about it all day. We can live without beauty, without artistic beauty, therefore without art, since there is beauty in nature, but we can't live without justice.

And all the mime plays that I'm thinking of have to resemble (I mean, taken together) a pyramid. There are a lot of things at the lower part of the pyramid, but they end at the top by a point, and this point, it's man. Always man.

When we look through history, and we see Aeschylus, Euripides, Sophocles, Aristophanes, Molière, we see in them the concern for justice and anxiety about injustices. That's what makes the grandeur of speaking theatre, that's what makes the grandeur of poetic verse.

Eventually it gets to the top, the idea of mankind, the human condition. Man whom we pity. And even when I construct a love duet, it's only about love. It doesn't matter.

For me, love is not the main element. I'm thinking of man. Man in love. This man is perhaps a woman. And this woman is perhaps a man. It doesn't matter. The human condition. You have to assume that the audience member is an idealist, that he is a humanitarian, that he is refined. You have to. It's for him that we speak. It's not for common-minded people, for petty-minded people. You have to. It's under these circumstances that plays are beautiful and interesting, and also that they end up enchanting even the common minded, because they too, when they go to the theatre, are not completely common minded.

There you have, I believe, the most important point of everything I have to say, because the rest are divisions, sections that contribute to what I just said. If the art in question had been sculpture, I would have liked to be Rodin; if it were dramatic poetry, I would have liked to be Corneille, and if it were theatre that's very well done, poetic, I would have liked to be Shakespeare – but one thing would not have changed: man, above all else. Abstract man above all else. And to speak only for a distinguished public. And this distinguished public, you see, I know who it is. It's me. When I create a piece, I create it for me. I imagine that I am in the audience, that I'm not a theatre professional, I say to myself: would I be moved by this piece? That's the whole question. The public doesn't interest me. You mustn't cater to the public. We go to a lot of trouble for the audience and there's no point. Whenever I've been audacious, the audience immediately accepted it. Each time that I was concerned about being close to reality, they didn't understand.

It's fashionable to speak of revolution; well, the real revolution is to do away with the audience, and that's what I do. And there's a reason why I don't think of the audience; it's that I don't know who that is. There are several audiences.

If we managed to have a view of the public, it would be a great conglomerate, a great mixture, it would be a little bit of what we call the crowd . . . so I don't try to please the crowd; in pleasing them I would be encouraging them to stay as they are. No, this would be more common minded [*vulgaire*] than trying to please the common minded.

You know that the word *vulgaire* is a word that has changed meaning despite its root. It's original meaning is 'a lot', 'everyone'. We still say today 'scientific vulgarization', which means within everyone's reach . . . and little by little the word acquired the meaning that it has today . . . if we try to please the general public, if we imitate that group, we can't win it over. We can't win over the people we imitate. We don't appeal to people that we congratulate. To win people over, you have to prick them on the soles of their feet – the only things we feel acutely are pain, insults, so we have to continually insult the public.

We have a good idea what the audience is capable of, and we especially see what it is not capable of; it's not capable of seeing the horrors towards which it is sliding like water.

And if you do theatre to make money, as Jouvet used to say, in that case, it would be better to sell peanuts.

What is, then, our hope? It's first of all that I please Etienne Decroux, that's my audience; if I please him, I am saved. They said to me: 'But how are you going to do that when you act? You can't be in the audience and on the stage at the same time, it's unfortunate.' Perhaps through film I will be able to be in the audience and on the screen at the same time.

But all the same, one would want to have people in the audience, and not just anyone. Who would it be if it weren't just anyone?

That makes me think of a song: 'Children of Bohemia, we like those that like us', but I wouldn't say that; instead I would say, I like people who like what I like. If someone doesn't like what I like, I don't like them. I don't like the person who doesn't like what I like. So then, first of all, me: Etienne Decroux. I perform for Etienne Decroux first. And here come people who like what I like, so already I am no longer all alone; there are people with me.

You have to practise an art form for people who like that. You mustn't practise an art form for those who, in a pinch, can do without it. You mustn't write verse for people who don't need it. It's not enough to serve good wine to someone; the person has to love wine. It's not enough to put a beautiful

103

woman in a man's bed; he has to love women. That's the first requirement. We invite people who like that. There are people who are happy to see a body moving without knowing what it means. Then, there are others whom that doesn't interest. You mustn't make concessions where this is concerned.

Is mime a necessity in our time and does it have a future?

Mime, and we have to start with this idea, doesn't exist. For mime to exist, there would have to be mime schools. There would have to be a number of them with students who would stay for five or six years and who'd study the way one studies music. Next you would have to give performances often and there mustn't be people going to see mime saying: 'Hey! What the heck is this?' One wouldn't go to see mime out of curiosity, but it would be like going to see an exhibit of paintings or a concert. So that I will think of mime, above all, as an art form: the art of beauty. So let's assume that it exists.

With regards to its future, we'd first have to establish that it not die!

That said, I don't think that it is particularly a necessity for our time. Why would I be a supporter of mime? Well here's the reason: it's because it was an art form which, from a conceptual standpoint, was crucial and they forgot to create it, to construct it, to make the statue of an art form that was of major importance. We can imagine the world of fine art like a cathedral with niches set aside for the statues. So we would have for example: the statue that represents line drawing, the one for painting, the one for music and finally, in the area of language, the one for literature. But where bodily art is concerned, I see that the niche is empty and that there is nothing inside it. They'll say: 'Oh yes there is – there's dance.' But dance isn't essential; it is more of an exception among the corporeal movements of man. How many times, I ask you, have you spontaneously danced during the course of your life?

I chose mime, which is the negation of literature, because still today I'm learning things and I am faced with new problems. Do you see the difference? By having difficulties, one senses the victory, the victory over the difficulties. When the work comes too easily, you're not as happy. You can't admire yourself – you can like yourself a lot (*I* like myself rather well!), but as for admiring oneself, that isn't conceivable. You can only admire someone else, you can only dream of an ability that you don't have, and when you shine a little in this ability that you don't have, you're happy. The moral is: let's avoid things that are easy.

I struggled so that Corporeal Mime would exist. That's because it didn't exist and also because it was lacking: we had dramatic breath in all the arts except with the body. Because dance doesn't have dramatic breath. We'll find out later if [Corporeal Mime] doesn't succeed, but it was worth it to try. There are some things that are lacking and others that aren't.

When you see the arts lined up next to each other, you might wonder what use each one serves. What is the supreme interest of each art compared with another? Why do they exist? I remember once, there was a man who said: 'Why do mime, since there is speaking theatre?'

Unfortunately I didn't know that he was a painter. Otherwise I would have said to him, since there is colour photography, why do you want to paint?

The great problem is not to create a beautiful mime play; I mean to design it. We can design a beautiful mime play fairly easily and with success assured, because it's an art form that does not yet suffer from competition. It benefits from being something new. People say to each other: 'Ah, we're going to go see that.' So, what is difficult? It's difficult to keep a troupe together. If I read Alexandre Dumas, *The Three Musketeers*, and someone said to me: 'It's extraordinary what they managed to do!' I would say: 'No, it's not extraordinary. What is extraordinary is that they managed to stay together.'

I'm thinking of that Greek, I think it was Archimedes, who said: 'Give me a fulcrum and I'll lift up the world.' Well, give me a troupe that continues together and we'll conquer the world. And that's the story.

Because it's also kind of easy to catch birds by first putting a grain of salt on their tails.

What I don't like in this question is that it seems to ask what the purpose of mime is. You can't ask what purpose it serves. We make things because we need them and making them satisfies that need. If we made a thing because it served some purpose, we wouldn't succeed. We should espouse a craft the way one marries a woman. It should be a marriage of love. We do it because we need to. And here the words of Jesus Christ come back: 'And all these things shall be added unto you.'

Figure 12 Eliane Guyon and Maximilien Decroux in *The Mischievous Spirit* (1947). Photograph by Etienne Bertrand Weill.

I forgot to cite this sublime statement which is, I think, from William the Silent: 'I will maintain.' That's extraordinary, because maintaining is continuing and man doesn't like to go to a lot of trouble to maintain; he still prefers to go to a lot of trouble in order to get ahead.

In mime, we have instances of the 'I will maintain', lively and intense immobilities, and sometimes in difficult balances, we maintain – we hold steady. This William the Silent, he said something else, and here, I'm saving the best for last: 'It is not necessary to hope in order for you to undertake . . .' – perhaps someone had asked him, 'What's the purpose of that?' – '. . . nor to succeed in order for you to persevere.' We can say that for mime, it's the same: we do something that serves no purpose and we notice that it ends up serving a purpose.

That's all. I did what I could to give you an answer, but I always have in my thought the fact that I might not be giving the response people expect. You ask me a question: I explain something to you that you didn't need to know. We find what we're not looking for. We find something else, and at least that's one thing found!

II On the definition of mime

You said that 'mime is the essence of theatre, which itself is but an accident'.

Yes. It's an apt turn of phrase!

Let's try to imagine, not historically – because we weren't there in antiquity – but logically, how one could go from what is said or from what is written, to what is done.

Let's take what we call the novel: close to it in form is the short story, but also the tale [*le conte*], and we know that in the countryside, for entertainment, there were storytellers that went from village to village. The villagers would welcome them warmly, the storytellers would sit down by the fire – it was often in winter – and, in front of a great many young people and farmers who came to listen, they would start to recount their tales.

What happened when we went from this action of story-telling to what we call the theatre? Well, instead of hearing a storyteller say: 'Achilles said this to Agamemnon,' we would see a human being who was portraying Achilles and who spoke as though he were Achilles. What do we see if we examine the thing under a microscope? What is most strikingly original is not the word, but a physical manifestation intended for human eyes. Because a man can exist without speaking; but he cannot speak without existing. It is therefore necessarily the body that appears first. The body is the essence, the body is what's new and it's the reason one comes to the theatre.

Next, what do you hear? The voice or the word? You have to make the distinction between the voice and the word and it's easy to sense this difference when one attends a play acted by a foreign group. When we hear a foreign language, it's first of all the voice and the diction that reach us, but one doesn't hear the words, because one doesn't know what they mean! People will say: 'But it happens quickly, it's [hearing and understanding] almost simultaneous!' No, it's not simultaneous. There is still an order of sequence and of causality. So that, in short, the first thing that comes to us after we leave the novel or the fairy tale is the physical body of the actor which is there for us to see. Second is the voice, and words only come afterwards. And since we know that it is possible, perhaps, to interest people through body movements and immobilities, we can say that the body is not the accident of the theatre. It's what they'll put afterwards that will be the accident, in order to make up for an inadequacy, for example. We also know that a man can be interesting with his voice, by producing sounds with it, like moaning or groaning, and, in this way, the voice can be an art. But if the producer of this voice, which is supposed to be artistic, isn't able to interest us, he's going to use a crutch – speech – that will intervene wherever the voice is inadequate, just as the voice must certainly have been introduced when the body was inadequate. That's how speech became dominant, and plays were written before being rehearsed. The word became lofty.

In its present state, theatre is not what I call an art form, but a kind of entertainment and it would be pathetic to think that it had become an art form and had ceased to be entertainment. Because now, what devastates me, what irritates me, is that one is in favour of doing 'interesting' things. This word, 'interesting', I have heard in all the countries where one gets bored! It's always in the countries where one gets bored that one does 'interesting' things. I'm not going to list these countries; you can guess what they are. They consider watching a performance a punishment, like a chore, like a scientific demonstration, and the worse it is, the more they find it interesting – which is, by the way, not stupid. They want to put their mind in a whirl and be among the small minority who understands things that others don't understand. And why then would I become refined myself? I have other things to do than to be refined. If I were refined, I would work hard to no longer be so. I want to move the people who work in factories and not move some sort of countess who adores all things obscure.

Take Molière, he wasn't refined. He's there, he resists . . . He said something, he showed something, he gave a lesson. And his lesson could serve us still if we were capable of listening to it. Molière, he is forthright. Reread the first act of *Tartuffe* and you will see this leitmotiv: 'The poor man, the poor man!' You feel that he's not counting on the audience members' understanding. It's not that they aren't intelligent, they are, but they are going to make every effort to misunderstand! There is that famous line in *Le Misanthrope*, said by one of the marquis: 'It's to you, if you please, that I address this speech . . .' That's the big question; the audience has to know that it's to them that the speech is addressed. And for that, you have to be forthright. You must be careful of men who say: 'I don't need it explained to me!' Yes you do! We need to explain it to you clearly, to be sure that you don't misunderstand that it's to you that this speech is addressed.

A critic who just saw *Brand*, an Ibsen play that's a bit similar to *Le Misanthrope*, wrote: 'And now we understand that it's no longer about admiring Brand, but about doing as he does.' And there you have it; it's not about being admired, but about inspiring people to rouse themselves to do something, to change things. Outside of that, art is only entertainment and I, for one, am not interested in amusing people.

In an unpublished text, you wrote:

> Mime consists of imitating with movements of the physical body, using the body of the person who is imitating. As with wine, you can serve it pure or with additives. Whether it imitates just a part of what one is depicting, while leaving it to the sound, the décor and the spoken word to imitate other things, or whether it imitates the whole thing, it does so only through body movements.
>
> Another way to say it: whether one produces it with music, musical sounds, décor, words spoken by a narrator, or by the mime himself, it remains an art of the body. The things that accompany it don't change its nature, no more than the female who walks near the male changes the essence of the latter, no more than the words that tell us the song that the music sings to us, changes the essence of the latter.

What is the nature of the mime of which you speak?

Let's say that above all, the art of mime consists of a cleansing, or, if you prefer, a purification. What is a cleansing? It's keeping only the essence of a thing. But you have to understand that, at the beginning, the word 'pure' is a word of the rational mind, and that is not a compliment. That means that it's an art, an activity that isn't mixed with another.

So you have to get it into your head that the idea of purity is a means and that it's not necessarily a guarantee [of quality].

Pure mime can be ugly, very ugly; there is even a great chance of its being ugly; and before knowing how and why, we must already have some sense of what pure mime is. It is a dramatic movement of the human body which is meant to be seen. If there aren't words, tones, scenery, they say that it's pure and that's quite verifiable.

Is he alone, this actor that one calls a mime, or is he given other assistance? If he is all alone, it's pure mime. That won't make it beautiful. We've seen speaking actors having a mime-like comportment when they acted, much more gracious and powerful than many mimes. So much so in fact that mime in a supporting role can be more powerful than pure mime.

And yet, one knows that I felt tied, right from the beginning, to pure mime. And I still am. But why? It's a process! That means, as in chemistry, that you must first empty yourself out.

In chemistry, you first have an empty crucible – the emptiness is important, it's what allows you to see clearly what is going to take place – and then a chemist comes along who is going to place a certain simple substance in it. Nothing changes. There isn't anything to say. He puts in another. Maybe he still has nothing to say. He puts in a third while removing the first, and the moment comes where an explosion occurs. He knows it's the combining of two simple substances, of a determined nature, that caused the explosion. If he hadn't proceeded as he did, he wouldn't know that.

So, in placing the mime on a bare stage, without sound or visual support, we have a way of verifying what the mime can do and also, we forget it too often, what he cannot do.

It's a way of discovering excellence, but in itself it's not excellence.

To mime means to imitate. You mustn't forget that the word *imitation* has not always been unfavourable. Today, it means to copy and also, if we want to be even more modern, 'to photograph'. In short, it means realism. You know that words, little by little, have taken on another meaning as a result of the way we've used them. How did the word *imitation* get reduced to such an extent? There too, when the thing happened, I wasn't there.

In the seventeenth century, they used the term *imitation* for what we today call *representation*. And already we see that there are representational arts, and that mime is not all alone, that there are also what I will call presentational arts. A presentational art is an art that consists of presenting something that doesn't represent something else. That's the case, for example, in architecture. A monument doesn't represent a monument, it *is* a monument – it presents itself. A piece of furniture doesn't represent a piece of furniture, a piece of furniture *is* a piece of furniture, it presents itself. Whereas representational art, as the name implies, is one thing that represents another.

So among the representational arts, I will cite first of all line drawing. I say *line* drawing because the word *drawing* is a word whose meaning is so vast that we don't know very well what it means. Next we have sculpture. Drawing is practised on a flat surface, and sculpture works in three dimensions. Then there is painting, music, which is a representational art in movement, and mime, which arrives last. That gives you five representational arts that one can call sensory, because they address the senses, to which we can add an art that addresses intelligence: literature, which gives us a total of six representational arts.

We are in the habit of saying 'dramatic mime' when we say mime. But dramatic mime is the portrait of what? We already know that we have desires as powerful as they are contradictory, and mime cannot speak in order to relate these interior contradictions. Mime is obliged to perform them. Now then, man carries a drama within himself long before being in conflict with another man: he would like it if one thing could offer everything; he'd like to be able to go to the left while going to the right. The body alone recounts this drama. Man is not in harmony with himself. But when all the parts of himself are in harmony, then he dances.

That's what distinguishes dramatic mime from dance. A dancing man is in harmony with the world. When I say the world, I mean everything that is not him, everything that is outside him. We don't see someone waltzing when they are in conflict with the world. If one is in conflict with the world, one resists it, one defends oneself against it, or one attacks it and we hardly know how waltzing would constitute an attack or a resistance. Also, within the man that dances, all the parts of his being are in harmony with each other. If he waltzes, there is no conflict. Whereas in the example I gave you, there is a conflict between two parts of myself. I've sometimes said: 'One can dance alone, but one can't mime alone.' I've said that very often. That can seem surprising, because we often see two people dancing together and we've seen a solo mime, and now I'm saying the opposite: one can dance alone, but one can't mime alone. How do you reconcile that?

First of all, we know very well that someone who dances with a woman can just as well dance alone, and the woman, also, can dance by herself. So, that's sorted out – we see them dancing together, but we also know that they can dance alone. The mime, if he is all alone, it's inside his mind that there are two conflicting forces.

'I hate a woman, for moral reasons, but I desire her sexually,' is somewhat Alceste's drama in *The Misanthrope*, and when they say to him, 'but Célimène has all the faults that you denounce', he responds, 'I know it, my sense of reason tells me every day.' But reason doesn't govern love, and he adds this: 'Her grace is stronger than the rest.' There you have man, he's not one, he is two. Alone on a desert island, he is already dramatic. You can think all by yourself, you can't mime all by yourself. If you were all alone, there wouldn't be any drama; there have to be two of you. But, on the other hand, for there to be two of you, there doesn't have to be more than one man.

The dramatic mime that I practise and that I advocate, we also call Corporeal Mime. I use my body as does a dancer and I oppose what I do to the old pantomime that considered the face and the hands of primary importance. It's perfectly obvious that the old mime had a body and that he used this body, but it's an incredible thing that when we see the drawings of old mimes, they always depict their faces or their hands. It's just as obvious that we have a face, hands and arms, but that we consider the body of primary importance, the main part of the body. That's a big difference.

When he saw one of my shows, a circus specialist said to me, 'You want to make an art form, from the outset, in the abstract and you don't build on the past, therefore it's bad.' So, I respond to this man: 'From the past and even today, to encourage us, we have statues!' The statue is not a mime that uses his body, but it's still something: it has a physical pose. So we weren't all alone on the earth and we didn't work, from the outset, in the abstract. That statue, we had to make it move, because it is an exhortation and it makes one want [to achieve the equivalent in movement].

If we summed up a bit what Corporeal Mime does beyond its exemplary nature, we could say that it does what it thinks, and the mime, as I conceive of it, thinks. But of what does he think? Well, of everything! If I want to sharpen a pencil, I have to think. I have to know where to get the pencil, where the penknife is, how I'm going to open it, and then, to pay attention. If I want to drink something, you can't pour a glass of water in my ear, but in my mouth and not on my tuxedo. When you scrub the floor, you think. You think to a greater or lesser extent, but you think all the time. That's why life works. Without that, there would be subway car accidents every fifteen minutes. Thought goes with us everywhere.

In everything that a mime does – and this is also something that distinguishes it from dance – he thinks. It's not possible to resolve a problem you're faced with while dancing; if one has a difficulty to resolve, one feels like sitting down and thinking. That's why when we speak while walking, to say something important, we stop. This thought is the stance we take when faced with a problem.

So, the mime thinks and what he thinks, he does. It's important, because in this case it's morality which is at stake. It's as if one were saying to men: 'Be careful, you are always sitting down and you're going to die from it. You are sitting at work, sitting at home, sitting at performances. When you die, we're going to have trouble putting you in a coffin because you will be bent in two from being seated. So watch out, do something, move!'

Humanity lacks action and it lacks seriousness. It doesn't lack ideas, but it's not enough to have ideas, they have to be realized.

So if it's true that a mime can't stir up a lot of ideas, at least he commits himself. Take a segmented movement of the body backward: you risk fracturing your skull when you do it.

A writer doesn't commit himself, a painter doesn't commit himself: he can erase everything and start over again. In French, in the judicial domain, that's called 'altering the ledgers'. Mime, then, has moral value.

The mime artist is concrete, he is there in three dimensions, he moves, he stirs, he is living and everything he does are actions that are necessarily concrete. We don't think that a concrete thing can create something abstract, but how is it that simple, concrete actions, putting the hand somewhere, getting up, etc., move us by awakening in us a whole world of abstractions? Well, it's because they are metaphors, and very often, mime is a backwards metaphor.

In literature, metaphor consists of having in mind an idea that we call spiritual and then giving it solidity, we move back towards matter to find an analogy; it seems in general that mime is the opposite: first it does something that we could call material and the audience has the chance to rise up to an idea that we'll call practically spiritual. A literary scholar will say of Diderot: 'He's a vast mind.' He thus set out from the mind to go towards a thing that presents itself to our physical senses. Things are vast in matter before being vast in Diderot's mind. Mime does the thing, and the audience, seeing the material thing, thinks of its spiritual analogy. That's why you shouldn't be surprised that we attach such importance to the portrait we make of the five senses (sight, hearing, smell, taste, touch), as well as to the portrait of the five appetites (eating – earth, drinking – water, breathing – air, making love – fire, sleeping).

We, who are mimes, have to try to make poetry through action and not through the word.

It's not enough to remove speech in order to do mime, but you can't try to replace the word's function, which is to describe things which are absent. Abstraction is absent from reality; the word tells that abstraction. Generality is absent from reality, the word tells that generality. A hidden thing, absent from our eyes or a thing which is very far away, several miles away, absent in space: words tell them. A thing that existed centuries ago, absent in time: the word says it. What will exist later, also absent in time: the word says it. All of this is perfectly obvious, but what is less obvious is that the word also says what is absent from our consciousness, even if it's right in front of our eyes. Our eyes are like cameras, they see everything, but our consciousness doesn't notice everything. It's the word that comes to tell us what we have to be aware of, and mime can't do that. It shouldn't try to do another's job with tools it doesn't have. An art form does not have to walk on its hands, it has to walk nicely on its legs and make what is easy, difficult. So mime is going to try to have as much charm as the word, but not in the same way.

Mime can't explain what is hidden, nor what is so far away that we can't see it; it also can't say what is yet to come and it can't say what is past. There are a lot of things it can't say; it's handicapped. Obviously mime can find consolation. It can say: I am not alone, painting doesn't do any more than I do, nor sculpture, nor music, so it's a consolation not to be all alone. Except it still has to try to bring a richness that the word cannot. It has to struggle to equal the word, but not to replace it.

In general mime becomes typical when it is, let's say, like a man who performs everything on the head [the top or cover] of a barrel. And from that moment on, we see that the most typical movement, not the only one obviously, but the most typical, is an inclination. And if we think of an inclination, a question presents itself: how far should we incline, and how far can we incline?

Of course you can't do the impossible, and that's not laziness speaking. I just mean that you can't go against the laws of physics. In an inclination, beyond a certain point, we fall. But you have to, at least, go up to that point. So they'll say to me: 'But why is it necessary to go up to that point?' Because it's possible. And when something is possible, there's a good chance that it's required.

Mime is like a pyramid on its point. You have to prevent, in Art, as everywhere, the *'between two'* – the in-between. I am vertical, and, well, one has to know that I am vertical and that that's what I intended. My body is on a diagonal, one has to know that that's what I intended.

Giving the example, doing something, and something that didn't come easily, that's the mission of mime. If mime does it, then people will say: 'He does it! So we're going to try to do it, too.' I think that's the most captivating aspect of mime. Mime is the most exemplary of the arts. Out of all the fine arts of representation, mime is the most exemplary. It rises up among the arts like a prophet. Mime is the only art that can say: 'What I think, I do. I am at once the subject and the object. I am the artisan, and I am also the material.'

He thinks, and his thoughts continue in his body. If a mime is stretched out almost naked on the floor, and then slowly he gets up, it's an example, it's an invitation to do the same. It puts us in the sphere of the example.

We can have a change of powers, give it to those who don't have it, take it away from those who have it; we can kill lots of people, exterminate the classes. We can do a lot of things, but what hasn't been done, is to place right there, on this table, a new man – not a new king, but a new man. A man who will find it completely natural, as though he wanted to regenerate the world, to think while moving!

Nonetheless, one has to add that in all art there is an opposite that characterizes this art. What characterizes painting is colour, but it also needs black. What characterizes music is sound, but it also needs silence. What characterizes a statue is the convex surface. From a distance, a statue is only a convex surface – it's a little like the Gallic monoliths that are only bumps – it's from close up that we see other things, the hollowed-out parts that emphasize the bumps. I think that we can apply this principle a bit with everything. And if mime, as I have conceived it, has to be above all an effort, a construction, a struggle to think or to get things taken hold of and to move them, there also needs to be some rest. In an undulation there are concavities and convexities. It's as if it's a law of life. If breathing is above all inhaling air, you also have to exhale. We find this everywhere. Mime, if it is typical, when it does something, when it constructs, it changes the world. Perhaps I haven't insisted on this enough. To change the world is to take hold of things and move them. That's how one changes the world and, moreover, that's how beds got built. The bed is a place of rest once it is built, but one doesn't rest in building a bed. One cannot rest before it's made. Man is dramatic, especially to the extent that he changes the world, and it's because there is struggle that there is drama.

Let's get back to this difference, which for you is fundamental, between mime and dance

But dance is a part of mime! Dance makes movements with the body. And these movements represent something. Dance too is a representational art, but dance is to mime what watercolours are to painting, what Savoy is to France: a part of the thing. And *our* mime [Corporeal Mime] is part of what? Of mime in general, of mime considered as a genre. So that will give us old-style mime that focused on the face, and ours that focuses on the body, and then dance, which we have to talk about. What similarity is there between old mime and us? It's that both are dramatic. And what similarity is there between our mime and dance? It's that both use the body.

Let's have a look at the differences to better understand. We'll see that our mime contrasts with old mime because it focuses on the body, and contrasts with dance because it is dramatic whereas dance isn't. I know dancers don't like what I'm saying here, but I'm not here to please people, I'm here to say what I think. So dance isn't dramatic. And when, under the name of dance one does drama, it's because it's not dance. And so what is dance? What are its depths? What do I think of when I say *dance*? I think of a semi-spasmodic movement. And why semi-spasmodic? When you dance, there's no question that you have to do so intentionally, and yet you feel that dance carries you away. You make a decision to dance, of course, but you dance a bit in spite of yourself. It's common with the waltz. This semi-spasmodic movement makes one think of a spring – something that goes down and then comes back up, without being able to tell when it stops going down and when it starts coming up.

One can't think rationally while dancing. There was a man who was not called Decroux but who was called Cicero, and whom we can take seriously, who said: 'No one dances who isn't simple-minded.' Which means that a reasonable and rested man can't dance. Suppose that you had an arithmetic problem to solve, would you try to solve it while waltzing? Certainly not!

The dancer is in harmony with himself and with the world. When one is dramatic, one is in conflict with oneself and with the world.

So are there still other characteristics of dance that are linked to this fundamental idea? We dance because we feel like it whereas we don't work because we feel like it. If we look at natural dance, spontaneous dance – because it's that type that counts and not artistic dance that tries to be natural – it's obvious that the duration of the dance conforms to our need. There's no danger that we'll dance for three hours when three minutes suffice. Whereas with work, even when we no longer feel like doing it, we have to continue because we're producing something. And dance doesn't produce anything. So what are we representing: dance or work? Obviously drama represents a task. Work and drama are almost the same thing.

There's another characteristic of dance, which is that it tends to repeat itself. Indeed, when something is pleasant, you might as well repeat it. As for our dramatic mime, it tends to do only one thing at a time, and without repeating it. And yet there are times when dramatic mime seems to repeat itself. Take, for example, the act of striking a nail with a hammer. Does the factory worker really repeat the same movement with his hammer? The first hit makes the nail penetrate a little, the second a little more and so on. It's not so much a repetition, but one strike for penetration, a second for another penetration, etc. Also, there is the fact that the force he uses is the amount that's necessary and not the amount he likes using. We see little by little the difference between what I call dance and what I call dramatic mime.

Now we need to have a quick look at possible confusions. In general the dancer's effort is with his body and the actor's is less so, just as the old-style mime's is less so. So people are going to make superficial judgements and say: 'That's old mime, because there isn't a lot of movement. Whereas that, over there, is dance because it moves a lot.' This accusation that we make of dance first came to us, by the way, from old-style pantomimes. For them, because we move a lot, it's dance. It has nothing to do with that!

When one wants to know if it's dance or if it's mime, it's not about knowing which part of the body moves, if it moves a lot or not very much, but rather *how* it moves. Whatever the body part, you'll have the spring [rebounding movement] of which I spoke earlier, or something else. And what is this other thing? It will be, for example, a quick movement, like an explosive one, followed by a stop, as though the man asked himself if he wasn't mistaken in making this quick movement.

He also needs time to think to figure out what he will do next. So sometimes it's a slow movement, it's as though the man were thinking while doing something else.

Athletes reflect. They are all dramatic. They aren't representational artists. They don't act out a struggle, they are the struggle and can't not interest a corporeal mime. But that's different.

So there is a difference between mime and dance, but also one between natural dance and artistic dance?

To start with, natural dance has become a suspect term. For some people, it will mean a spectacular dance, but one that is inspired by nature.

In a natural state, when we're not watching ourselves, we have the vestiges of the prenatal shape. But where does the natural start? To understand the natural do we have to return to prehistoric man and walk bent over, as if we were going to fall onto our hands? Is nature the fact of going back to being a monkey? And assuming that we're going to go back to the monkey, why not go back even farther? Why not call what comes later 'natural', rather than what comes before? Thus prehistoric man would be less natural than the monkey. It's very hard to know what we mean by 'natural', but, on the other hand, we know what today's man does when he lets himself go to what he feels is his nature: he lets himself go!

In sports where there is a great need to be strong we readily assume the natural attitudes that are inspired by the foetal position. There is not a big difference between the racing cyclist's attitude and that of a child in his mother's womb. It's also the case with skiers. One night when I was running, because I was afraid of missing my subway – and it was serious, because I would have had to cross all of Paris on foot – I noticed that little by little I had taken on the prenatal attitude: my legs closed in, I was leaning forward with my whole being, my feet fell flat on the ground. I was exactly the opposite of what I wanted to be.

So there is a theatrical dance that is inspired in part by so-called natural attitudes. And this dance that is called 'natural' is going to fight against turned-out legs and lots of other things. Classical dance, on the other hand, fought nature because classical dance imitates a character that it considers ideal from the point of view of civilization. We can debate about this ideal, but one thing is certain, we cannot confuse civilization with nature. Civilization is a struggle against what we don't like about nature. It's a discipline. It's resisting doing everything that we want to do.

Classical dance is a good thing because it is the culminating work of a biped and because it symbolizes civilization. Condemning the classical is to condemn two-footedness and civilization.

We see two-footedness in verticality which is the main characteristic, because the biped is, above all, a being concerned with being upright. If for example the leg bends in classical dance, it's so it will straighten better, it's not in order to stay bent. There is also in this verticality a certain something that makes the chest seem to present itself like a face, as if the breasts were eyes.

Why does one become bipedal? To see farther. To see is to foresee. To be bipedal is to be civilized.

And if we observe civilization and research its components, we see that there is first of all strength, then the mind, then goodness and finally happiness. Strength, mind, goodness, happiness. If these don't exist, we see it as a lack. It's what we are hoping to realize in civilization.

Let's look at strength: it's possible to think that strength is a rather bestial thing, but in acrobatics, in fact, we see that strength makes what is heavy, light. Human strength is in conflict with earthly gravity; it is praiseworthy.

Next, the mind: this is first of all satisfied by the taste for geometry. To love geometry is already to love reason. It's the fact of going from the simple to the compound. In classical dance we find this taste for the rational. Let's look at an example: I studied classical dance as a student, and I observed it with great care. And I think that all movements in dance can be reduced to two. We'll have first of all caressing a disc – the leg seems to caress a disc – and next it caresses a cone. Isn't it marvellous to think that with these two movements, the caress of a disc and the caress of a cone, they've made ballets for three centuries that have earned the public's admiration?

Let's continue: the trunk, horseman of the legs, thinks that he doesn't help his horse carry him, because they say in ballet that the trunk ignores what the legs do. There are simple-minded people who thought that the ballet dancer forgot to use his trunk, whereas he works hard not to use it. When a man is silent, that doesn't mean that he is mute or that he has nothing to say. The trunk is like a horseman and the legs are like the horse. That satisfies the mind, because it's the symbol of the mastery of man over nature. 'Man makes blind matter serve him,' said Victor Hugo.

Next the pyramid on its point: that's still the mind. In general, the two legs seem to be joined together. Obviously there are times when you have second or fourth position, but . . . in ballet, if one opens one's legs, it's in order to close them again; if one bends the legs, it's in order to straighten them. Here we find again the biped who wants to see in the distance. The idea goes even farther . . . sometimes there is only one leg, and the other leg serves as a third arm . . . that's still in the realm of the mind, because this is how the widening out of the bouquet and the pyramid on its point are done. It would be impolite, wouldn't it, to offer flowers with a widening out of the stems rather than the blossoms. No, the widening out is done above. And so if one imagines a pyramid on its point, it's a victory. And these symbols, what are they symbols of? It's the reduction of the volume and the weight of the cause, without reducing the volume and the weight of the effect. It doesn't destroy the idea of the cause, even though we know that man also wants a world without a cause. But since there can't be a world without cause, he wants to make a world where the causes have less volume and less weight.

Next there is the sliding step. This step means that man has managed to destroy the obstacles on the ground. The ground is horizontal in all directions, it is flat, it is fixed, which is not the case on a boat.

Pointing the foot indicates the continuation of the line. That too is part of civilization. Everything that is born wants to grow and everything that grows wants to live.

Next the opening of the leg – not to be confused with the opening [turning out] of the feet when the legs are closed (one couldn't walk like that) – is the symbol of the opening of the mind, and there we have the mind satisfied once again. If opening the leg isn't a symbol of opening the mind, what are symbols? What do we have to do to satisfy our enemies?

Now let's look at kindness. I could have said *altruism*, but my grandmother didn't know what altruism was; she used to speak of kindness. I always try to speak like my grandmother in an attempt to escape the influence of 'intellectuals'. So, then, kindness: imagine a little boy sitting on the ground. He has his back towards me. If I want to make him slide along the floor using the pressure of my foot or if I want to kick him as punishment, but without hurting him, my foot will have to make contact in the following manner: the toes of the pointed foot will turn out and it's the bottom of my foot that will tap his behind. It's an example of another opening that is a sign of kindness. If my foot hits his bottom as I just explained to you, I hurt him less, and if out of playfulness, I push him to make him slide, ditto. So the turning out of the leg is a sign of kindness in the case of applying pressure or striking. It's also a symbol of the opening of the heart. We don't have only the mind; we also have the heart. If I hold a wallet between my knees and open my legs, it falls. That means that I already agree to someone coming to take it from me.

Now let's look at the walk in classical dance. This turning out of the leg and of the foot in walking is the sign that we are interested in what is to the right and to the left, and not only in getting to our practical goal. It is practical and economical to go right towards one's goal, but it's not beautiful. Everything that is profitable is not beautiful. But if on the contrary my leg goes forward, and if while going forward, it looks towards the side, it moves in the direction of what's practical while looking towards the unnecessary: that's a sign of kindness. Rather than thinking only about getting to one's bank, man is thinking that there are little birds over here, or a nice young lady who is shaking out a cloth over there. It reminds me of a song by Charles Trenet: 'Hello, hello swallows, there is joy. The sky is over the roofs, there is joy.'

It's precisely that, to the right, to the left, to the right, to the left . . .

But let's get back to the pyramid on its point. It's a sign of kindness, because if I am threatened, I need to be a pyramid on its base. And if I want to attack, it's the same, I am a pyramid on its base. But as soon as I am a pyramid on its point, I am vulnerable. It's a sign of civilization to accept being vulnerable. I know that they could push me, easily make me fall, I know it, but I'm not afraid. So this pyramid on its point that we said was a metaphor for the mind, to extend our vision, also designates kindness. Here I don't see very far, there I see a little farther, a little farther, a little farther . . . it's foresight, but it's also kindness, in that one could easily pull me to the ground. I live among people who are as civilized as I am.

Now we come to the last component of civilization: happiness. If happiness is not always as we would have it, it's nonetheless happiness that we want. We have the right to be happy when we've been good. There's something remarkable in ballet; it's the concealing of effort. When the dancers have to walk, they always say to them: 'Smile, smile.' If you don't look as if you're suffering, the audience feels comfortable. And once again here's the turn out of the foot and the leg, because in this walk, not only do I have enough kindness to be interested in the right and the left, but I enjoy it. As the dwarfs in Disney's *Snow White* sing: 'Whistle while you work, tra, la, la, la . . .'. That's happiness. The walking man goes in a particular direction, it's his work, but it doesn't prevent him from looking to the left and to the right. Not only out of kindness, but for the pleasure of living. It reminds me of a sentence by André Gide: 'I don't like to choose, because choosing means giving something up.' And indeed, if I choose, I relinquish things on the left and the right – all over the place.

There you are. I've sung ballet's praises, rational praise. No! I spoke to you with calculated dryness. So now, I'm going to speak of its faults, but while being careful to add that none of them is essential. They aren't part of its essence, but are, as it were, of an accidental nature.

The misfortune is, you see, that the purest man, the most virtuous, is under the influence of the world in which he lives.

A saint in a bordello, well, eventually . . . and the world is a bordello . . . Ballet, also, is subjected to this influence, is ashamed of its virtue, excuses itself and little by little becomes a bit depraved. Dance's weakness is to add a little of what pleases the crowd: quantity and story.

Let's take quantity first.

The ideal would be to have a quantity of quality, because if we're talking about gold, it would be best to have lots if it. However, there is still the danger that in wanting to satisfy the need for quantity, we might offer copper in place of gold.

Let's take the [ballet step called] *entrechat*. If we want to do a lot of them, we will be at the *entrechat*'s mercy and could very easily tense up. It would be better to do fewer *entrechats*, but, as far as the concierge is concerned, it's quantity that interests her.

Next there is the number of turns. It would already be beautiful to do a single turn, and to stop, balancing on the foot that pivoted. Unfortunately that's not what happens. In wanting to give quantity, one is going to want to make several turns, and at the end, one is going to wind up on the other foot. It's nothing but an athletic success without anything artistic about it. It's so difficult to stay on the pivoting leg, still to be on that leg when you finish. As we turn, we lose our balance and feel like using the other leg to stabilize ourselves.

Overworking is also a part of quantity. Instead of having a pleasant smile, one has a smile that becomes forced. Those are just a few examples of the damaging effects of quantity.

And now, the story.

In watching a story ballet, we ask ourselves: 'Is this dance, or is this mime?' We are not completely satisfied because stories are not told well by dance. The bit of mime that there is in this dance has not found its full expression. It's quite obvious that in its natural state, dance doesn't lead to story-telling. The need to dance is not the need to tell a story. I speak perhaps in order to tell about something; I can use gestures to tell about a piece of work, but I don't dance in order to tell about anything. I dance because I enjoy it, that's all. It's only from a decision of the mind that one dances a story. It's because one has decided that it would be so. Now then, when one prefers a story to the way something is done, it's one of the characteristics of cultural ignorance. Our daily life isn't artistic, but it has a story. So we'd like to be told an even more condensed and interesting story, stories like we see on movie posters: guns and naked women. (People who make the posters know about men, they know with whom they're dealing.) But to appreciate the 'how' [rather than the 'what'] is to discover the symbol and that makes a real art consumer, someone who doesn't need a story. He sees the symbolism in the movements, he discovers analogies – one thing makes him think of another.

Another disadvantage is that stories don't allow one to show all the beautiful things that are available to us, because the opportunity to include them has to be there. To be able to put something in a story, it has to be appropriate. If you have a beautiful thing which is not appropriate, you have no right to put it on the stage.

And finally, above all, there is the danger that the story is a written one, conceived by a writer – who is sitting down.

A story for people of taste is conceived by a seated man. It reminds me of the army during the war, when there were seated men who were deciding if there should be an offensive: 'At such and such a time, the men will leave the trenches and charge. And there mustn't be more than 10 per cent who die.' Up to 10 per cent would be acceptable – and [those men in charge] continued to be sitting down. It's the same for someone who conceived of a ballet. You wind up with something like this: 'There's a man whose soul has been stolen. He tries to find it, and when he sees the person who stole it from him, he makes him understand that he has to return it.' We call these 'noble subjects'; it's stupid, these are people who don't understand the business.

Regarding ballet, there's a marvellous thing. And that is that dancers who don't have a powerful personality can all the same belong to what is called the corps de ballet. It's thanks to them that there is an architecture on stage.

To look at a cathedral is beautiful, and the stones that make up a cathedral are modest. If these modest stones didn't exist, there would be no cathedral. But if each stone said: 'I have a personality! I am a cathedral!' you can imagine this cathedral that would be represented by cathedrals piled on top of each other! There would be little holes because of it. There are skin diseases like that, where one has holes all over.

To finish this discussion of dance I'm going to tell you an anecdote.

They asked the famous sculptor Carpeaux to make something beautiful to put on the pediment of the [Paris] Opéra: The spirit of dance. I don't know if it's he who came up with the title, or if it's the government who imposed it on him. I have no idea. He, then, made this group that one can see when one comes out of the Opéra métro station. These women are beautiful; they are not classical. It's rather surprising. Inside the building they do classical ballet and the statues they put outside are anti-classical. They asked Maillol, another famous sculptor, what he thought of this work and he made this idiotic, crass response, even more surprising in that he was a very refined person: 'It's good, but why did he sculpt kitchen workers?' But of course they're cooks, and that's why it's good, because their opulent bodies are raised up by the spirit of dance. This proves the strength of this spirit which raises up bodies that are made to stay in one place.

In mime, should objects be shown or should they be mimed?

The first idea that comes is to mime the object, to evoke it with mime without showing the material object. And that's how I started, I might add: climbing a tree, swimming in the water, so many things . . . it was material, material, material. I first imitated things from what I call *Primitive Life*, then the imitation of *Artisanal Life* and finally the imitation of *The Machine*. I called these *The Three Ages*.

It's fairly instinctive, as soon as one says, 'I am going to do mime,' one wants to imitate. And why would one start by imitating the manifestation of feelings? The first reflex that comes is to imitate the materiality of objects and actions.

But after this spontaneity comes another justification. Speaking theatre – do I need to repeat it? – has speech. Through speech, one can tell of things that are not there, things that are not present in time and in space. One can say, for example, 'he's working' and as soon as one stops talking, it's fairly natural to show the work itself. And it's rather nice to see. Why? Because what interests us in the world are not things, but Man. But the fact is that there are advantages, but also difficulties: one cannot evoke everything with perfect accuracy.

There is one thing that escapes us, above all else, and that is colour, or the details that are within things. Van Gogh was happy to make portraits of his shoes. He was right; those shoes are poignant. Through all the details of the shoe, we think of struggle, of age, of ageing. And if we manage to evoke a pair of shoes, we couldn't put in this imitation all these moving details. We can evoke fruit, but we can't evoke its colours. Then there's something more serious than that. It seems as if things tend to resemble each other and here we find ourselves threatened by what in mime we call homonyms. Instead of seeing an umbrella, a cane or a sword, we see mostly a long and not very thick object. Instead of seeing a grapefruit, a soldier's grenade or a ball, one mostly sees a sphere. These are some difficulties and limitations. Obviously one can, by context, make it understood that it's about a sword and not an umbrella. But there isn't a context that would allow one to guess the colour and the touching details of an object.

Little by little one realizes that there are things that one prefers evoking rather than seeing them and others that one prefers to see rather than evoking them.

Then there is something else: props risk cluttering the stage. We are not making movies. We can't lower the curtain every two seconds. It's thus desirable for us to evoke the props that get in our way.

In evoking props in mime, man has to be the negative mould of the thing. So, for example, look at my hand, it provides the negative mould of a sphere. We shouldn't imitate the sphere. It would be funny if someone who were offering an orange put his fist in the shape of an orange! Who would eat this orange? So mime has to show the negative space of the object.

Take the action of climbing a tree and imagine a realist director who would have a tree brought on the stage – you have to be ready for anything from them! – this would not be a very good idea.

We know that in many cases, it is man that's beautiful. You have to focus on man and not get distracted by the thing. But it's just that that doesn't work every time. It depends on the story that one is telling. Take for example a letter that announces some very bad news: you'd need some pretty fancy mime to get across the idea that a man is a postman and not a butcher boy and that he's truly bringing a letter and not a calendar. Next someone opens the letter – there can't be a mistake, it has to be well mimed – and the person has a violent emotional response. What disproportion! What interests us in this case is the emotion, and we had to make an entire pyramid of mime to get across the nature of the evoked object, which, in fact, gets used very quickly. That's an unfortunate thing, or rather a limitation.

We mustn't be strictly doctrinal: there are cases when one must evoke an object, and thus not show it, and others where it would be better to show it. There is not just one remedy for all sicknesses.

Sometimes we join together the two procedures and I am going to explain what we did for the meal in *The Little Soldiers*. I had asked the actors to have real plates, a real dish of food and a certain number of real things. I told myself that we would remove them eventually, but that in the beginning it would be easier in order for me to see the architectural movement of the scene. But we couldn't actually put real liquid in the glasses. Why put in real liquid? It's pretty easy to make people think you are drinking when you already have a glass. So you already see the coming together of the two approaches, there is a glass, but no liquid. We rehearsed like that, and, little by little, we realized that it worked well. We even realized that we could make percussive music with the metallic plates. You see that in this case the two approaches came together. A happy marriage.

I had a friend, when we were relatively young, who said: 'You see, it either works or it doesn't.' Should you or should you not put a tree on the stage? If it works, you should put it there and if it doesn't, you shouldn't. He was right, and he was wrong to be right so early on. You must go through the doctrinal phase, the rigour. You can't be reasonable too early on. You have to go through the phase of having a set idea, it establishes your credibility, and afterwards, you really have to give some flexibility to your intelligence. Doctrine, to start, can be a stimulant for thought, but later it can become an excuse for laziness because we leave it to doctrine to think for us. Doctrine should help us think but should not exempt us from thinking. That's what too many mimes do, 'Mime must do this . . . mime must do that . . .' You must leave the doors open. You don't know what can happen. You can't let it slide towards laziness or decadence, and something that allows us to better see what we're doing is not decadent.

When we created *The Trees*, it was the actors who played the trees. That's where the poetic ambiguity comes from: to divine a tree through a man. Glimpsing the tree through the man. And if we glimpse one thing through another, that's already poetry.

From a moral standpoint, there is something else to add. When we make it a rule to imitate a prop – I mean, to evoke one – or to imitate a practical material action, it's work. After all, it must look like what one wants it to represent. The concierge has already seen swimming, has already seen climbing a tree; the concierge knows a lot of things and if you don't do your work well, she can tell. Whereas in the expression of feelings, one can't prove that it's real. You can always say: 'I see it like this and if you don't understand it, it's because you are an idiot. For me, emotion is like that and you can't prove the contrary. It happens in the unconscious.' And the unconscious, that sells, it's a good product; they sell it in the Monoprix.[7]

But with material actions, we have to discipline our body – and there is a poetry in material actions – that's natural.

There is a moral doctrine above the activity of men.

To interest my concierge, do I, as a mime, thus have to have impeccable technique?

There are many who say: 'I don't have to do anything to shine, to be worthy, to be glorified, to be at the top of the hierarchy. I don't have to do anything, I am – that's enough. The incarnation of the verb "to be", is me!' Not only do they think that they don't need to study technique to perfect themselves – since one can't perfect something which is already perfect – but in addition, they say to themselves: 'Even if in the night, by an applied scientific process, they could insert in me, have penetrate into me, knowledge that I don't have, I would consider it a rape. They don't need to make me better; I am perfect. I am. You are going to deform me.'

As though one could *de-form* what is already without form!

A mime should not hate technique. He shouldn't feel that technique disturbs, suffocates, strangles inspiration, but on the contrary, that it helps, exalts and refines . . .

In a pair of shorts, you have two pockets. In the right pocket, there is a little white marble cube that is called technique, and in the left pocket there is a little white sugar cube that is called inspiration. The man in shorts swims across the stage. When he has finished, in the right pocket they find the little white marble cube and in the left pocket they don't find anything. The little white cube melted. That's the story of technique and its relationship to inspiration.

Technique allows one to experience personality. It is an obligation, a language and it says to us: 'You have to do like this and not like that.' Technique gives us orders. It eliminates mediocre performers, uses average talent and exalts genius. It allows us to distinguish between personalities. Whoever is able to express himself despite technique proves the power of his personality.

Technique is the possibility to do physically what one conceives of, at least what one believes one is doing. To acquire technique, the struggle is long, because the body betrays us.

Mr Paul Bellugue was a professor at the Ecole des Beaux-Arts. He was fascinated by his work and we used to see each other once in a while to exchange ideas. One day, he said to me: 'Technique is the hand's obedience to the mind.' I was struck by the clarity of this reflection. And we can say that in Corporeal Mime, which is our art form, technique is the body's – the whole body's – obedience to the mind. Ah, this is no small thing! Because it happens that all the movements one *wants* to make are not the ones one *should* make.

We like the vertical because that relaxes us: we can rest more in a vertical position than we can inclining to the side. We like the horizontal because that relaxes us. We also like the diagonal because it is in the middle and because each thing – it's logical – has two extremes and a middle. And the *middle*, that's the thing. There are thus the audience's demands, driven by the geometric spirit which wants the balance we find in all the arts. All arts have the principle of balance first, whether it be architecture or music. And that doesn't prevent expressing powerful or subtle feelings. Balance doesn't bother them at all; on the contrary, it helps them, it exalts them. So we must overcome our nature, our habits – habit is a second nature, we have habits and we have form – so that the body obeys the spirit of the consumer, the spirit of audience member. Also, the first spectator of mime is the self, he sees himself, he judges himself, he wants to improve, but these improvements are always against his body's nature. There's the struggle! The corporeal artist is at war with his body. He doesn't want this natural way of being, this second nature thing, or even habits, which we call a second nature. He doesn't want nature. He wants to have just the nature needed so that the spectator has the pleasure of seeing to what extent he is still manifesting his nature, all in trying to reach the ideal.

The artist that produces must always stop himself from time to time to see what he's doing. So he feels, he senses that he is himself an audience member sitting in the room. That's what he must do.

In the artist there are two men, one who does and one who sees if it's well done. It's not the same man. They don't have the same demands. We can even say that their demands are contradictory.

When I was in Milan, there were two buildings. Technique was studied in one of them and, in the other, which

was a little theatre, they did improvisations. One day I crit-
icized the students for not attributing any importance to what
they had learned in the technique building when they were
doing improvisations. One of them said to me: 'Oh, are we
supposed to do like we do over there?' That's revealing!
Indeed, if it's about acting like ordinary actors, one could
wonder with good reason if it's really worth it to study
technique. It reminds me of a student who is now a television
director, and who said to me one day without realizing what
she was saying: 'You have to admit that they don't like things
which move around a lot.' Imagine this poor individual that
we call the actor, man of *action*, who is there, and at the
moment when he's supposed to really move into action, the
director says this very well-known phrase: 'Whatever you do,
don't do anything!' We realize, little by little, that it's really
exhibitionism. No! Let's say instead that it's an exposition.

We mimes represent, all the same, a revolution. A con-
structive revolution. No! After all, it's maybe not a revolution,
it's maybe just a construction. We had dance that used the
body but wasn't dramatic, but the body in service of drama is
something we didn't have.

Where this gets complicated is that the very beautiful
[technical] figures that we study and call *technique*, in truth
are poetic lines that we construct, they are not poems. Imagine
that the most beautiful lines of poetry were written on little
bits of cardboard, and that we threw them out of an aeroplane. People would pick them up and say: 'They're beautiful.
But how are we going to use them? How can we make a poem
out of them?'

The technical elements [or figures] that you study are just
poetic lines. So when you create a story of your own, you are
necessarily going to draw from memories. There are lines that
you'll take, and others that you leave behind because the story
doesn't need them. The great advantage is that often what one
does not find through inspiration, the lines bring to you. This
technical figure brings us a feeling. If we had started from this
feeling, we wouldn't have found this beautiful figure that
expresses it. It's the figure that brings us the feeling on a silver
platter. We make a figure to work out a technical issue, we

133

make it more beautiful, we find a logic, first it's scholarly, but when it's finished, it's beautiful. And afterwards, not only is it beautiful, but it means one thing and not another. When working from the inside, we don't find anything.

On that subject, we've already had a conflict between two men who were separated by around two centuries: Boileau in the seventeenth century and Théodore de Banville in the nineteenth. Boileau said: 'You first have to have the feeling to have a line that expresses the feeling, and then you find the rhyme afterwards.' He admired Molière and he said: 'How do you do it, Molière? How do you so easily find the rhyme?' Théodore de Banville, who wrote *L'Art poétique* in response to Boileau, said: 'No! First we find the rhyme, then the line.' For him, the rhyme is a physical fact that allows one to find the moral fact, which is the line of verse.

One idea leads to another, and speaking of poetry makes me think of how I've sometimes said that there's something miraculous about a line of verse. A line isn't really miraculous, there's no such thing as a miracle. But I mean that a line of poetry seems miraculous. When we hear verse, it seems like the thoughts of a man falling from the lips of a god. It's a divine language used to say things that are not divine, that are human. We could, if we were set on using this term, say that it's divine in the sense that it's above man's ordinary state.

Versification is like the soul's vowel.

But I have something else to say. Imagine all these figures that you have studied, that we call technique, sitting like people in a big amphitheatre. They are there, there are hundreds of them, and you are there, you are creating a story, and you sense that there's a particular feeling that you want to express. Then there is a figure that says to you: 'You don't need me?' So you say: 'But yes, I do!' You wouldn't have found it on your own. There's a whole crowd of figures that are ready to help you. So there you have the feeling that attracts the figures and the figure that had created the feeling. Do you see this means of picking up what we need [from a storehouse of technical figures]? I'm doing a certain type of exercise which is a figure; I discover a feeling. And next, you have a man looking for a feeling, and the [technical] figure comes to mind. Well, there you'd have something really special!

And it's the same thing with mime: if you created a very beautiful figure, a complete one, people would go out of their way to see it. But it happens that in a mime play, this same technical figure distracts them. That is why you have to consider reducing the figures. Taking a figure that reflects absolute beauty, that is to say as full an expression as one could imagine, full like an egg, and keeping the principles that brought it to life, but reducing it so that it becomes more modest, more discrete. But to be able to reduce a beautiful figure, you first need to have constructed it. I can already see actors who would be sitting among us and who would use this as the basis of an argument in order to find any way they could not to have to work. They would take advantage of what Chaplin said, 'Mime is immobility.' They would say to each other, 'I am immobile. I understand the work of the actor and the mime because I am immobile.' It's not so simple! There we would have someone who would say: 'You heard what he said, you have to reduce the figures because they are too beautiful! Well then, I might as well just be myself since I don't have any range.' That's not it. The figure must be completely expanded before it is reduced so that the quality within remains.

Despite all that I've just said, we are still called to create our theatre. A school teaches technique and the art of beauty but it doesn't teach passion.

Let's tackle the main technical principles of mime now

There are three things in which a mime must be perfect: in its breathing, in its articulation and in its rhythm. Certain technical principles follow from these three things.

When I say *breathing*, you mustn't think that I'm referring to the pulmonary breathing they talk about so much. This breathing, described by bespectacled theoreticians, who reflect and then tell you what a lung is; that it's there that it happens, that sometimes it fills up with air or lets air out, and that we breathe like this: 1, 2, 3, – 1, 2, 3. The great misfortune of these theories is that once you're on the stage, they're of no use. When I performed in *Ancient Combat* some years ago, I did almost the entire piece without breathing. As Seneca says, 'Everyone is a pilot when the sea is calm,' and we always breathe well when we don't have anything to do.

No! I'm speaking of something else. I'm speaking of the philosophical sense of the word 'breathing'.

If they put a sublime show on the stage for us, we couldn't take it for long. There have to be contrary things in succession so that they breathe, and us with them. After the peak of pain, we need the valley of rest.

Now let's look at articulation. Articulation is making syllables, which are composed of consonants and vowels, following one another, without them getting mixed up. There are actors who speak very quickly and yet who have very good articulation, and we don't miss anything they say!

Jacques Copeau, for example, used to give dramatic readings. During these, he read to us from Sophocles, Aeschylus, Euripides, Aristophanes, Plato and of course Molière, Corneille, Racine and Victor Hugo. Sometimes he had to speak quickly, very quickly. And, something that may seem contradictory, he spoke quickly the way others speak slowly. Despite the speed of his delivery, we could clearly identify each syllable.

The mime artist, then, also has to articulate, because he has the analogue of syllables, and even the analogue of vowels and consonants. All of that has to be very clear: one should feel where the thing stops and where it starts and where it finishes.

From there we get the principle of doing just one thing at a time when we want to be understood. If one doesn't want to be understood, one does several things at once.

Alas, this principle of 'one thing at a time' immediately encounters a pitfall – one can't find the absolute. It's the same problem in wanting to transform the body into a keyboard, which is one of the other important principles of mime. It's an intention, but it's not possible. With a piano, one can isolate notes from each other, but with the body one cannot. And yet our goal is to resemble a piano keyboard. We shouldn't be surprised by this; in a lot of areas, there is a goal that one knows will never be obtained. I've heard Christians say tha Christ should serve as our model, and yet they know full well that we could never be like him!

Let's take an example. If we want to perform a sequence of movements very quickly so that it looks like the movement of a snake, we will say: head, neck, chest. If we had studied the three separately, instead of it being just anything, it will be a curved movement that will have a certain quality. In piano studies one says, 'detached notes' and there is another study that we call 'linked notes'. For things to be linked, they first have to be detached. You see that we are the sons of Reason.

Let's tackle rhythm now.

Rhythm exists in all self-respecting arts.

If we take music, it is rhythmic even when it doesn't seem to be. There is music to which we can't walk, dance or sing, and despite this apparent absence of rhythm, everything is counted and there is a rhythm.

Architecture is, of course, rhythmic; instead of being rhythmic in time, it is in space. The building blocks are distributed rhythmically.

With sculpture, the rhythm is less obvious, but a statue is far from being rectilinear and there is the idea of the vowel.

In painting, too, it's not so obviously rhythmic. There are colours that weigh on us, that push on our solar plexus, and others that spread out into the air. And, well, there is a rhythm between the pressure of some colours and the lack of pressure of other colours – as if there were another plane, an undulation.

The audience needs rhythm just like it needs rest. So we, in mime, also have to have rhythm.

That brings us to the *choc*[8] and to the 'stop' that's going to lead us to the subtle combination of elements.

I mean that the stop leads us to the continuation. If we have stopped somewhere – for logical reasons, in the construction of a technical figure – well, when we make a continuous movement and pass by the point where we had stopped previously, we have the memory of this stop, and it's not the same thing. When an express train passes a station, it doesn't stop but it knows that it's a station and that the station was invented for stopping. So it goes through this stopping point knowing that it isn't stopping. That's not without significance.

Now let's consider the *chocs*. If we proceed by *chocs* in a study, like for example the seahorse's tail (which is a sort of arm undulation), there are nine *chocs*. And so when we perform the absence of *chocs*, we will remember the *chocs*. And in this way, throughout the whole seahorse-tail exercise which imitates something very rounded, very continuous and soft, we have the character of the real seahorse tail, because in the movement of the exercise there will be the memory of the stops and *chocs*.

Let's go on.

There is another advantage to stopping: if we make an explosive movement, the audience does not see the path traced; it sees the bodily position before and then the one after. It's time that's going to allow us to realize, to understand, and that takes us back to the principle of 'one thing at a time'. That's important because mime is pretty much the only art where people don't know what to look at. Here you have one actor who is doing something and another who is going to do something else: which one am I going to watch? When should I stop being interested in this one man in order to watch the other?

It's one of the weaknesses of mime, a blessed weakness because all arts are disabled. It's what forces them to use their intelligence. Painting doesn't have movement, statuary doesn't have movement, music is not visible, etc. Each art does something great because it is disabled. Thank goodness, we don't only have *this* disability. If we take a man by himself, he is, in spite of everything, a little bit like a group. Should we watch his feet or his head, his eyes or his hand? That's where the 'one thing at a time' becomes necessary so that one doesn't get distracted.

This brings us to slow motion.

The word 'slow motion' comes from a process employed in cinema when they want to show the route followed by things that moved quickly. Slow motion is a means of representation. But what does it represent?

If we take a practical perspective, we can say that slow

motion plays the role of the microscope. There are things so small that one can't see them with the naked eye, and the microscope allows us to see a reality that hadn't reached our senses. Slow motion allows us to see the path that we hadn't identified because the course was followed too quickly. Thanks to the slowness, we can see the route that the thing travelled. Thanks to slowness, we see how the thing occurred. Knowing it is a question of honesty. It's a truth that one is seeking and it's a truth that gets revealed. And it's not negligible – if something has moral value, there is a good chance that it has artistic value. With my experience, I know that there can be honesty in art, and not just greater or lesser emotions. Slow motion is beautiful. But is it truly beautiful? Rodin said: 'Slowness is a beauty.' Perhaps it's not beauty, but a way of verifying beauty.

Slow motion seems to me to represent paradise. For me, paradise is not a place of pleasure, but rather a place of happiness: happiness as opposed to pleasure. Pleasure makes me think of a hydraulic dam: the water accumulates, can't get through, finally it does. Accumulation, pressure, bursting. After pleasure: a temporary death.

Slow motion, on the other hand, doesn't represent pleasure; it represents happiness, serenity. If there is a tremor, it's a continuous tremor in a continuous slowness. Paradise is not a place of active verbs; it's a place of the verb 'to be'. Slow motion, this slow movement, doesn't go anywhere, it's not in a hurry, it goes by while we linger. It's a travelling version of the verb 'to be'.

Slow motion speaks to us of honesty, because if a movement is not beautiful, we see that. It's a confirmation. To do movements slowly that we normally do quickly is a bit like lighting up the night.

It's just that nothing is simple, there's no formula making things easy. That's what's unfortunate and one could very well say that slow motion is boring. And why would it be boring? Because we know beforehand where the thing is going to wind up! It makes us want to say: 'Get on with it, let it do its thing!' If we approached things superficially, we could say that beauty is boring. This is not simple!

Perhaps you know it, but I didn't know it until recently, there was a thinker, a great thinker, and so of course he was Greek, from ancient Greece, who said: 'We grow tired of everything, except understanding.' That means that we don't get tired when we are in the middle of figuring something out. But if we understand right away, we'd really like the sentence to be short. So should we use slow motion or should we not? They tell us that it's beautiful, that it reveals beauty, but that it's dull. What should we do? There are several solutions, and among them is not to be too slow. Slowness on stage is the portrait of slowness in life and we can give an idea of slowness without causing boredom. Next, if we have a rhythmic musical accompaniment, what was unbearable becomes bearable, or even enjoyable. Next we have line breaks. If I walk in a circle with equal slowness for a long time, the audience is going to get bored because it's going to see where I'm headed; it's already going to have understood. But if I make a fraction of the circle and then I head off in the other direction, and then in another – slow motion but with changes in the line of direction – then we would have the advantages of slowness without the disadvantages. Furthermore, slow motion doesn't have to last a long time. We can imagine alternating between fast and slow-motion movements.

Let's remember Chaplin, 'mime is immobility'. So mime would be alive like the sun. From our perspective, the movement of the sun is hardly noticeable. We don't see it dancing, we don't see it oscillating, and yet it shines and heats us. It is alive without moving; it's marvellous. It's often the impression we have when we see certain photographs. I remember the photograph of Einstein. When he died, I was in Oslo and the newspaper vendors there published a little poster of Einstein's face. It didn't have to move to send us spiritual rays. It's also the case with the speaking actor. When he acts intensely, he doesn't move: he speaks and peoples the space with his words. But in mime, that's not the case. So, when we want to allow ourselves to be completely still, you already have to have a face that seems interested enough and is therefore interesting. As Victor Hugo says: 'There is no dazzling being who is not dazzled.' An immobility can be longer or shorter depending on one's face and whether it looks more interested or less inter-ested. The Bible says that God said to man: 'You will earn your bread by the sweat of your brow.' *We* could say that we earn our face by the sweat of our thoughts.

Having said this, mime is an art of movement. So what must we do? Should we move or not? It's like with slow motion, a solution must be found. On the one hand, we will have immobility or stillness. Next we'll have an explosion, which will give us an immobility before and an immobility after. The advantage of the explosive movement will be that we won't see the moving from one spot to another.

One can't imagine that someone can go from one spot to another without making movements that constantly modify the previous bodily position. And if he is transported without a jolt, keeping his form, one can say that it's 'transported immobility'. Someone who takes a trip around the world in a plane, and who falls asleep, that's a transported immobility. With regards to the Eiffel Tower, it travels quickly, very quickly, because it turns with the earth. And yet the object itself doesn't move at all: that's a transported immobility.

That brings me naturally to the subject of dynamo-rhythm.

I don't like new words, especially when they are scholarly words. I like it when we have new ideas, but told with old words, and not that we have old ideas told with new words. Now there is a deluge of new words, but we don't really see so many new ideas. Words hide thoughts, or rather the lack of thought. Sometimes it makes me think of a beautiful shell where there's nothing inside. So if it's like that, why did I choose the word 'dynamo-rhythm'?

To make sure I'm properly understood, I'm going to sum up the elements of our art.

First there is the part of the body, the thing that's going to move, that will be moved. Will it be the head, the arms, the leg? That's something to consider, because each body part has a particular virtue. We can't completely forget that the brain is in the head.

Next there is drawing, that is to say the path the body follows. If this path had left a trace, it would be a drawing.

Why did I say drawing? Perhaps I should have said movement. But movement is already complicated. In the idea of movement there is the idea of mobility, of the driving force, of the verb *to move*.

Whereas drawing is like a line left behind by a thing that has moved. In short, a drawing is a bit like a road, and on a road lots of things can happen. There can be a lightweight automobile or a tank; things can go quickly or slowly.

After drawing we have speed. In French, the word 'speed' has a meaning that varies according to the context. It can mean fast, or, in another context, the time that is taken for a determined route. In this case, one can speak of slowness as a kind of speed. What speed does an automobile go? Slowly. Whereas the word 'fast' means a moving from one place to another in very little time. One can't speak of the slowness of a rapidity, but one can speak of the slowness of a speed. There is thus speed, more or less slow or more or less fast. Inside, we can put stops of whatever length and, up to this point, it's like music.

We have then the part of the body, which is the instrument; drawing, which is the intonation; speed, more or less slow or fast; and, finally, force. Force is a rather surprising thing. In an art intended for the eyes, force is extraordinary. How do we know if we should show force? We can see which body part moves and [identify] its itinerary. But can we see force?

Force is like electricity – we can't see it and yet we can tell it's there; we can infer its presence.

How?

When a muscle is used, it changes form. The hollows are more hollow, the bumps are more bumpy, we feel clearly that something has changed, something that's visible. We know force can be sensed rather than being visible.

So, why the word 'dynamo-rhythm'? We could have made do by saying 'speed and force'. And yet they're so tied together that often we need to use the word 'dynamo-rhythm' which means [elements of speed and strength] 'an interweaving'.

Bad news, good news bring about different responses in the body: these are dynamo-rhythms. Passion is first of all dynamo-rhythm. It's a luxury when an animal can move about; there are animals that can't move at all. Their only responses are contraction and release: that's dynamo-rhythm.

Yes, dynamo-rhythm is what most intensely expresses passion.

In the technical work of mime, there is a fundamental element: the counterweight. What do we need to know about that?

'Counterweight' is a word that exists in our everyday language, but that has, it's true, a rather technical meaning in our art. It's the art of giving the impression that one is pulling or pushing against 'something' but this 'something' [does not exist]. It's a difficult art. Let's talk about this difficulty.

If we lean against a wagon to push it, the thing is simple to conceive of, but if the wagon isn't there, it's more difficult. The same thing is true if we pull on the wagon.

But what is difficult? Is it to imagine that the wagon is there when it isn't? No, it's more complicated than that. Obviously the work of the actor consists in imagining what doesn't exist. That's his job, and the mime too, being an actor, a dramatic artist and not a dancer, has to be thus able to imagine what doesn't exist. And it's not very difficult to imagine a wagon that he intends to push or pull. The difficulty is in the following: when we push the wagon, our whole body is inclined towards it and it is likely that our bent legs straighten. But if the wagon isn't there? Logically, we should fall. There lies the difficulty. We can't do a counterweight without going towards an unstable balance that brings us to the brink of falling. With pulling it's the same. If I want to make it look as if I'm pulling, I might fall because I have to lean in the other direction. And if we don't do this and still want to make it look as if we're pushing or pulling, then that's amateurish mime: we do false counterweights in terms of inclinations and we try to make up for it by making contractions that are probably going to look pretty bad, contractions that can travel – in their contagiousness – all the way up to the neck.

When a counterweight is correct from the point of view of the balance and the degree of inclination, you don't have to have an unattractive contraction. It's something remarkable, and it's a good thing, since we all know that we shouldn't show unattractive effort on the stage. Imagine that we are pushing a wagon. Our front leg is bent; our back leg is straight. In reality, our front leg could have its foot lifted off the ground because it's not supporting our body-weight, it's the back leg that straightens, well rooted in the ground in order to push the wagon. In mime, the opposite phenomenon occurs. This front leg that is bent isn't free, it holds up our body, and the back leg that is straight doesn't do anything. The situation is reversed. In our art, the leg that in reality is free is busy, while the other one, which should be working, is free. It's the opposite. We can say that in mime there is what I call 'muscular drama'.

In life we make certain expressive gestures that complete our speech or increase its strength. We do them with such spontaneity that they must be very old. I think that one of the dominant things in prehistoric man was the [use of] counterweights. It was almost his life's regimen. And the use of counterweights as a dominant activity lasted well after the prehistoric period with the slaves of antiquity, the serfs of the Middle Ages or with the artisan. And even today a big part of humanity still works using counterweights. We Westerners are fortunate: our job is above all to try to discover just where we'll need to press our index finger in order to call for the elevator. But all the same, in speaking or in thinking, we sometimes make counterweights that don't serve a purpose. They are vestigial.

Counterweights, although in reduced form, accompany the speech of an orator.

I'm going to have fun and say that the first drama to assail man, and even animals, is the problem of weight. Indeed, when we push something with the intention of moving it horizontally, as is the case with a wagon, we don't have a horizontal support [perpendicular to the earth]. Whereas a little boy who wants to have fun, lying down on the floor, will push his feet against the wall to propel himself. So he'll have his horizontal support in order to move himself horizontally. It's the same for the swimmer when he arrives at the end of the pool: to turn around, they push off the side of the pool, a horizontal support [a support perpendicular to the earth], in order to continue their trajectory, which is a horizontal one.

Unfortunately, to push a wagon, that's not the same situation. Our push-off point is the ground and [it would be helpful if it were] vertical. What to do? We manage, despite the difficulty, by inclining the legs. Ballet dancers know what a *sissonne* is. The legs which are bent on an inclined plane, straighten on this inclined plane. Why don't we slip? Because the ground is rough, we grip it, and we can do this: we push while having the legs on an inclined plane. We make do with that. But when there is black ice, we can't push the wagon because we slide. This proves our fundamental weakness.

Man runs into a problem as soon as he wants to transport himself. What would a man be who couldn't transport himself? With this truly dramatic difficulty, we seem already condemned: we want to push things on the horizontal plane and yet we don't have a horizontal support [a support perpendicular to the earth].

Here's another generality to show the importance of counterweights: everything has weight. It was with the counterweights that I started the study of mime. Everything has weight. It's rather astonishing that I had the instinct to feel the importance of counterweights without really having thought it through. At the beginning what struck me the most is that everything has weight. What does that mean? How can we give a little bit of life to this affirmation? Not everything is round, but everything weighs. Not everything is pointed, but everything weighs. Not everything is hot, but everything weighs. Not everything is tender, but everything weighs. And it's astonishing that when I realized that everything weighed, the idea didn't come to me to back it up with the simple fact that the earth attracts bodies and it's because the earth attracts bodies that everything weighs. You see the full import of what we call counterweights.

Now we have to explain a little more specifically what counterweights are for. When it's a question of depicting manual labour, the work of a manual labourer, it's undeniable that for that task you have to know the counterweights. To show a combat with spears, which is still a kind of work, it's very obvious that you have to have knowledge of the counterweights. Without that, everything is wrong. What is more, these counterweights must be very fast, which makes things even harder. There's no need to press the point: we understand very well that for all manual work, for everything in the realm of the physical, in the realm of production and destruction, you have to know the counterweights. But what we don't think about enough is that they are good for something else.

We have in us vestiges of counterweights. We still retain traces of our past as prehistoric man, when, above all, we had to struggle with matter, and therefore to use counterweights against matter. In this distant past, we were engaged in physical actions, and today when we do certain movements where we don't need this technique of counterweights, we realize that traces of it remain, nonetheless, in us: mime is like an echo of distant things. We have moved from the indispensable to luxury.

I am going to clarify my thought. Let's start with laziness or grace. There are beings that have grace in their movements.

They tell us that grace is facility. We could also say the same about laziness, and that brings us to this idea that there can be unpleasant grace and pleasant grace. But let's look at this grace. Here's a man who has to lift something that doesn't weigh a lot, and he doesn't need a big counterweight. He doesn't need to make a huge movement and yet he does so. He's going to lift a basket of potatoes as if he were lifting something that weighed 20 kilos. Let's understand each other: there won't be any contractions but there will be the movement in space that there would have been if he had moved something heavy. It's like a movement of laziness and grace.

Now, having explained the first function of counterweights, here we have grace! Harmony is a way of making all the body parts collaborate for the benefit of one of them, not to wear oneself out excessively in one part of the body, but to make everything collaborate. Let's not forget that laziness was celebrated by the poets and that it's rather nice, except when it goes hand in hand with the love of glory, in which case it's only pretension. When we see a cat close to the fireplace, we know that it's lazy, but we appreciate its grace. Just let's not forget that the cat is not intending to run for President of the Republic.

Let's leave grace and go on to something else. When a man, out of passion, performs a concrete act, he behaves as though the object he is supposed to move were heavy. Let's imagine a man who has to take out the fountain pen that is clipped to his breast pocket. It's not hard to do, using only the force of the hand or wrist. And yet, if he is in a passionate state, he's going to behave with regard to his fountain pen as if it were a question of something heavy, or firmly attached. That's how passion expresses itself. 'Drive out the natural, it comes galloping back.' And our old nature returns in our acts as soon as we are impassioned, moved, angry or vehement. Sometimes, it's out of kindness: in order to say, 'To your health', we raise our glass as though it were heavy. Obviously there's no contraction, but we make little counterweights all the same, as though this thing were heavy. If we examine an orator, we see that he's speaking, of course, and that he's making gestures. It goes without saying. But if we observe him more carefully: he's pushing or he's pulling. He's pushing against something and this something is an idea. He pushes this idea as if it were material. Afterwards, he pulls on something as if he were pulling on his listener to attract him to an idea. He does counterweights without knowing it. He is like Monsieur Jourdain in Molière's *Le Bourgeois Gentilhomme*. Which proves that an actor should know how to perform counterweights as well.

To be over and done with this subject, I will say that when we really know counterweights, we prove, in knowing them, that we're professional mimes.

I suddenly thought of another principle: making circles with squares. If you like, make a beautiful circle, square it off and it will be beautiful. But if, right off the bat, you want to make a circle that doesn't have any memory of a square, it will be poorly done. At the Opéra there was a dance teacher, who, while she was teaching the *déboulés* – a big travelling movement which looks like a spinning waltz step – asked her students to make a square. 'If you make a circle it's not beautiful, it's mediocre, we don't know what it is. Travel by making square shapes to give the idea of a circle.'

You have often used masks. What importance do you attribute to them?

It's important, from the outset, to make a distinction between the inexpressive or neutral mask and the expressive, or character mask. At the Ecole du Vieux-Colombier, the actors made their own masks. And they strove to make them inexpressive. This way, if we were interested, it was due to the actor's talent and not the sculptor's talent.

What is character, then? It's obvious that it's easy to confuse character with the expression of emotion. Character is the crystallization of a dominant or determined feeling. Let's take, for example, pity. Everyone has felt pity; nobody has a monopoly on it.

A character can have pity as a dominant characteristic, and it's a crystallized feeling. However, he will not seem to be permanently in the throes of pity; he can also be happy or sad. But we will find one emotion that will be dominant – pity. The character is something indefinable, a bit like the rhythmic part a pianist plays with his left hand while the right hand is playing the melody.

Is the expressive mask good? It is perhaps good, but it's dangerous. Imagine a mask of amazing craftsmanship. Someone who plays the role of a wicked man would already have evil on his face. It's troubling, and it wouldn't take much for lazy people to get what they can from it; we wouldn't know whom we should applaud, the sculptor or the actor. And yet, one feels that if the actors were full of good will and hard working, there could be expressive masks, provided that the sculptor's talent didn't take over. Masks bring a bit what words or printed titles brought to silent films. Words were used to exempt the actor from miming those things which weren't interesting or which would take too long to mime.

I remember the period when I made a mask for myself out of a fencing mask on which I had embroidered eyes, a mouth, etc. That wasn't a very good thing. I gave demonstrations for a maximum of five or six people. I remember one time when someone said to me:

'But why do you have that thing on your head?'

'It's so that people don't expect facial expressions and so that their gaze is focused on the body.'

'Oh, right! But it's a shame, because we can't take our eyes off that mask!'

It was very disappointing and I wondered if one shouldn't use one's own face, making it inexpressive – if that wouldn't be better. And then I wavered between using and not using a mask.

What does the term *neutral* mean? There is something about the neutral or inexpressive mask that lets the actor interpret all possible feelings without being ridiculous. If I can represent joy and anger, rest or the need of activity, dying or sleeping, without anyone perceiving a clash between the mask and what I'm doing, if this mask gives me all the possibilities, even the most diverse and contradictory, without seeming ridiculous, then this mask is the neutral mask. A neutral or inexpressive mask – we have to tell it as it is – is sublime. Sublime doesn't mean that it's good. It's almost a technical word. In this case, sublime means that you don't have 'a man' before you, but rather 'Man' in general. And if that weren't enough, more than Man in general, it's Man from another world or another planet. And even more than Man from another world or another planet, it's Man who left his tomb to tell his life's story. Not just Man in general, but Man from all time, from the beginning of time to the end of time. That's what I call sublime: beyond all boundaries.

There's something else: with the mask, we see the body as a face. In other words, obviously, once we've got used to this mask, right? But the body-as-face is an extraordinary story. It means that we forget the man; we only see the body-face. That is to say that the corporeal figure appears almost abstract. It's already like a story of the man, separated from the man, as though we had extracted the figure while throwing away the man. And since the bodily figure almost always has symbolic value, the beauty is that much greater.

Masks don't only have the advantage of making us forget facial expressions. And mime masks, depending on the angle from which they are seen, offer a lot of variety. We lose the variety of facial expressions on the one hand, but we gain the variety offered by the viewing angles. Put yourself in front of a mirror and have fun changing the viewing angles: lean forward, back, etc. Do everything that you are going to be called on to do when the audience is there. You will see the changes of expression and will say: 'But we can do just as much with our uncovered face as we can with a mask!' Not as well, because there are fewer planes. One can design a mask as one wishes, with facets, so that each movement is like so many wake-up slaps in the audience members' faces. It's a resource full of potential.

The advantage of the mask is dazzling, and it has an extraordinary quality that's not even of an aesthetic nature. It has a moral quality. It's pretty sad to think that someone who had tremendous abilities for mime couldn't show it because he didn't have a face that an audience would like to look at. He would have a gift for tragedy, but would make everyone laugh. There we feel an injustice imposed on the actor.

Here's another example: a man looks old and he wants to express youth. He is hampered. Can he change the expression of his face enough to carry this off? I don't think so. I don't see how a person with very low eyebrows could convince you that he has very high eyebrows. How someone with a weak forehead can make us think that he has a domed forehead. It's very difficult to transform the character that is announced by the actor's face. Here, then, is a moral point. For it to be proper, the actor, who is a creative artist, should have the same rights as other artists. In other arts, the artist shows what he wants and not what he is. Rodin was a powerful and portly man, with a plebeian head, and that didn't prevent him from sculpting delicate, young, distinguished women. It's the same thing in all art forms: when we are in the presence of a work of art we are unaware of the physical appearance of the creator.

And that's precisely what true personality is. My personality is not the face that I happen to have; it's the face that I *want* to have. I am not what I am, but what I want to be. This is not a meaningless phrase, or the pleasure of saying a paradox, because deep down, if I want to be someone else, there's really a certain me who wants to be another me. A

Figure 13 Etienne Decroux in *The Factory* (c. 1946). Photograph by Etienne Bertrand Weill.

disinterested me, an idealized me, the best me of my several selves. So thanks to the mask, you forget what I am, and you think of what I do: therefore of what I want; therefore of my ideal; therefore of my true personality. If I have a crooked nose, due to an accident, or almost no hair, you're not really going to tell me that that's my personality. So I have the duty and the right to hide this accident, to put in the foreground my desired personality, because it's the damaged part of my personality that's hiding my personality.

During one period, you said: 'Mime is no longer mime if there is music.' Since then, in some of your pieces, music has played a part. Why?

Very early on I was opposed to the use of music. When I started to do theatre, I said to myself: 'What should we do in order to have pure theatre?' Obviously I arrived at this idea that it was the actor who was the essence of theatre; he was the new thing on the stage: the thing that we hadn't yet seen, and, as a result, theatre should be based on him. But, all the same, I imagined that the actor would need some help. To be sure about it, to really know what the actor cannot do, I said to myself: let's put him on the stage naked, in briefs, and let's not let anything come to help him. No special lighting which would provide him with a poetry that is not his own; no costumes, no words and, for a time, no shouts and no music.

I had something against music that was specific: I accused it of not being dramatic. I have never been a music lover but I liked march music and lullaby music that is clearly rhythmic. I enjoyed it. I quite like to hear a waltz. I always like hearing a national anthem, I am moved, it gives me shivers. But there is also meditative music that one doesn't feel like walking to, that doesn't rock us to sleep, that doesn't have an obvious rhythm, where the rhythm is known mostly by this Certified Public Accountant that we call the orchestra conductor, and this music, dramatic in its intentions, because of its hesitations, its surprises, its irregularities, really appeals to the music lover.

There is a thing that I don't like in music – it's the sound that seems pleasant to me, which is anti-dramatic. And we use music for so much. I'm thinking of a line of Boileau in *Le Repas ridicule*: 'Do you like nutmeg? We've put it in everything.' We could say the same of music. One wonders where on earth we could hide so as not to hear music. There is music tied to anything and everything. It's enough to turn your stomach.

So it was I who came up with this idea: mime without music. Because, before me, there was music. There was even a theoretician who wrote a fat book, during the time of Jules Janin, and who said you could not do mime without music. And I said: 'Mime is no longer mime if there is music.'

When I came up with this idea, I didn't know that it would wander around out there and would eventually come back and hit me in the face. Obviously I had good reasons for saying it, but they were insufficient. When one throws an idea out there it makes me think of that athletic game that we call *fronton basque* where you toss a ball against a wall and it comes back to you. I just made the statement off the top of my head, a statement against everyone, and when I used music, people said to me: 'It's not mime, because there is music.' They threw that line back at me everywhere, from Rouen to Göteborg! I would never have thought that I could be so honoured that my ideas would travel so far in space. Things travel quickly when you're not expecting them to!

When shouldn't there be music? If there are important events, music is *out of place*, it disrupts. It's as if one poured syrup on something that should stay bitter; as if one used an electric polisher on something that should stay rough: it's altering the pungency of things. On the other hand, when there isn't an event, when there is only development, then music is pertinent.

Is *The Carpenter* an event? I don't think it is. We know perfectly well that work starts at one end and finishes at another. We cannot allow ourselves to screw in a screw if we have not already made a hole for the screw or, to take it further, if we haven't put the screw in the hole. You have to take hold of the screwdriver before screwing; we cannot do these actions in reverse order. Things come as they jolly well have to come, and when they happen, we aren't really surprised and, in this situation, it's appropriate to use music.

153

Yes, music brings a certain charm. It doesn't heighten the charm of the mime, but it adds its own charm to the mix. Why does it bring this charm? Because in the action, when there isn't an event, the movement that is intended for our eyes isn't as captivating, as appealing, as intoxicating as things which are intended for our ears. The ear is much more sensitive than the eyes.

If you scratch a plaster wall with a nail, the line that you get will never be as moving [to the observer] as [the sound produced by] hitting a saucepan. For a line to be good, for it to move us, it has to have a certain form, whereas a sound produced by a blow immediately has an emotional power. Sounds are beautiful in and of themselves: as soon as they're emitted, it's almost a work of art, it's moving. That's what I think about music; it makes mime palatable. What was cold becomes warm. It's not mime that did that; it's music.

However, you have to be careful. One mustn't be ridiculous and choose a piece of music that has a melody that's too noticeable. It has to be a melody that one doesn't notice: one has to be taken, more than anything, by the pulsating rhythm, as in certain Bach preludes. If the melody is noticeable, it contradicts the gesture's melody and that's a drawback. That goes without saying. It's as though two people were speaking at the same time. And if the melody intended for the ears resembles the one intended for the eyes, it's very practical for comedy but it's ridiculous. The arm mustn't rise and lower in the same time as the music: a mime is, after all, something other than an orchestra conductor.

You need to be careful and choose music whose beat works well for the piece. In the age of silent film, there were projections without music, and the sound produced by the little tic tic tic of the film rolling around the spool made it seem to us as if that sound divided the immensity of time. It was nice, because man needs time to be broken up, just as he needs space to be broken up.

Obviously, it is prudent that the mime piece be entirely constructed and have its rhythm established before putting in music. Music must come afterwards, definitely not before. If it comes first, and we do mime on top of it, well, that's guaranteed decadence. It's lying down on the mattress of easiness. The music must come as something in addition, like a varnish on a beautiful piece of furniture. It's *in addition to*, not *first of all*.

In summary, when there are events that follow each other, you mustn't use music, and when it's a development, where there isn't an event, music is appropriate, provided that it is above all a beat, and that the melody is not apparent.

There you have the drawback of an improvised talk, but it's its charm as well. It goes without saying, I should have said this important idea sooner: which is that thanks to music, we manage to make the slowness acceptable – that slowness that so attracted me. But slowness has one drawback. It is sometimes appalling. Slowness bores people and slowness is beautiful. It's time to say: thesis, antithesis, synthesis. Thesis: slowness is beautiful; antithesis: slowness bores people. We need to find the synthesis: mime can very often manage on its own, but even so, with music we are saved. A slow gesture, that could be boring, is fed, so to speak, as if by an alcohol, by the music that accompanies it. We are not eager to see it end.

And so, through the association of ideas, I remember a remark from Rodin. He was in a boat – with a woman, of course – and at a certain point he said: 'Oh, I understand. Slowness is a Beauty!' Obviously slowness is not a Beauty, but slowness is a way of knowing Beauty, of becoming aware of it. But here's the thing: it also happens that once a gesture is started, we know where it's going to end up, and we want to say, 'Just finish your gesture, and let's be done with it.' Things are not so simple, but we know, from observation here and there, that sometimes slowness bores people and sometimes it charms. So music comes in like a bandage, like a healer, and the slowness is able to exist without boring anyone and have, as its only function, to charm.

You chose the seahorse as the symbol of your work. Can you explain the reasons for this choice?

I don't believe I am the only one to be attracted to this animal that we are reluctant to call a fish.

That said, why did I choose this animal as the symbol of my activity? What link might it have with our art of Corporeal Mime?

I come back to Chaplin's observation: 'Mime is immobility.' We're already coming close to my seahorse when it doesn't move through space. I agree with Chaplin, but I won't say it the same way, and I even think that he didn't express his own thought well. He would have done better to say: 'Mime is moving in place.'

There is such a thing as moving in place. The giant Atlas doesn't move . . . and who would dare say that he is immobile? There are forces at play inside of us . . . we already know that blood circulates, that air circulates, so why not force? A little like the sap that rises in trees, it isn't visible . . . but one can sense it. Actors who do mime with tension give a different show than those who act without any tension and yet, they will follow the same itinerary; they make the same designs with the same body parts. You can put them next to one another; they do the same thing as far as the moving of body parts is concerned, the same thing as far as the designs that one asks these body parts to make. But one is tense; the other is not. One is intensely present, and the other is just there, as though he were resting. Do you understand? We don't see the force; we have no way of seeing the force.

Mime is moving in place, and, it goes without saying that I'm speaking about mime when it is typical, because it has to move, the mime has to learn all the steps in ballet, without exception. He can't leave out even one of them. The most he can diverge from this is to invent a new step but he can't forget even one of the steps from the whole of classical ballet technique. He has to move intelligently, he has to choose the step that works best, etc. And in general, really, the mime moves through space.

Can we call it movement through space, the fact that the feet stay put while the upper body leans to the left, to the right? A bit like a tree. One hesitates, we say no . . . honestly, no . . . that's not it . . . and yet we are attracted to this definition: mime is movement in place. It's movement within exterior immobility. It's as if man were a shell inside of which things happen that we can sense without being able to see them. There you have some important points and I can feel that I'm getting close to my seahorse. And the mime artist has a means: it's what I call immobility transported. Since the word 'immobility' was used, let's keep it, out of respect for the memory of Chaplin, but this immobility gets transported.

We know very well that the Eiffel Tower is immobile, but when the earth turns, it has no choice but to turn as well. We have a clear sense that this is a transported immobility. We could give numerous examples.

There is something that is immobile in any case, something that is static; and that's a certain view of things. We could experience this with an automobile and a camera. We'll see that it's the same show: if a forest of sticks passes by me without my moving, or if I'm the one who is moving in this automobile with a camera passing by this forest of sticks, it's the same show.

Figure 14 Snapshot by Yves Marc of Monsieur and Madame Decroux, on one of the few vacations they ever took, in Thiézac (Cantal) in July 1974. The hotel keeper asked Mr Decroux why his daily walk always followed the same path, and he replied, 'If I take a different path each day, how will I know if anything has changed?'

Figure 15 Snapshot by Yves Marc of (from left to right): Jean Asslin, Madame Decroux, Georges Molnar, Denise Boulanger, Monsieur Decroux, Claire Heggan, Michèle Renaud-Molnar. This photograph, taken in 1974 in the basement classroom of the Decroux's modest cottage, shows a convivial moment with advanced students who served as teaching assistants and performed creations set upon them by Monsieur Decroux.

So we keep coming back to this thing: the thinking man is immobile. And when he seems mobile, it's because he's transporting his immobility.

Now then, the seahorse, when, precisely, it doesn't move, is a thinker. Its head is inclined downward, the way we do when we're working and even, especially, when we're analysing. Analysing does not prompt us to look up, but rather prompts us to look at the whole, the panorama of a thing. But if we want to understand it and know it, we feel like taking it in our hands, putting it on a table looking at it to be able to modify it, or, as they said in the eighteenth century, to divide it up. So the seahorse seems to be looking at something and we feel that its neck is in service of its forehead.

All the same the seahorse must move a little. I have already imitated its movement through space. It's very difficult, but it's beautiful. It's the end of the tail that moves a very little bit. And this brings us to the definition that I sometimes give: 'The mind comes from the eyes, style comes from the feet.' And for the seahorse, it's the end of the tail that moves a little, and there you are, its immobility is transported, without strenuousness. Someone who wasn't looking carefully would never have seen this little movement of the tail. And it seems as if the tail is like the beating of an angel's wing. It's extraordinary! The more we watch the seahorse, the more we are won over by it!

He's a thinker. His thought comes from the top of his body, of course, which moves thanks to what he uses for a foot, a little movement of the tail that undulates gracefully.

Notes

2   *Translator's note*: Decroux is speaking of the oppositional – dramatic – play within each thing: the 'un-dancy' quality that made it drama. Immobility was dynamic, not static – there was an inner movement even though the outside was still. The explosive movement had to have an oppositional pull for it to be able to end in a clean 'petrification'. The slow-motion movement was even because the oppositional forces balancing forward and backward movement were *almost* equal – forward motion won out by a hair and that close relationship in those forces was maintained so that the movement glided without accent.

3   *Translator's note*: The word for pupil/student in French comes from the verb for 'to raise' (as in 'raising a child'). In other words, the word *élève* implies someone who is going to be 'raised', 'brought up', 'elevated' – taught, instructed . . . someone who will submit (*se laisser*) to a

process that brings them to a higher place. In English we lack this lexical connection between *élève/élever*.

4   Perhaps Decroux had read these words: 'The artist must be, in his work, like God in creation, invisible and all powerful; we feel Him everywhere, but we don't see Him.' Gustave Flaubert, letter to Mlle Leroyer de Chantepie, 18 March 1857.

5   *Translator's note*: untranslatable pun where the third stage in the dialectic, *synthèse*, is replaced by a term which means 'bullshit'.

6   *Translator's note*: from the Celtic culture of Brittany.

7   *Translator's note*: popular French discount department store.

8   *Translator's note*: the French word *choc* means 'a jolt as the result of an impact'.

3 From *Words on Mime*

[Sections selected from Etienne Decroux's *Words on Mime* (*Mime Journal*, 1985), translated from the French by Mark Piper.]

1

Sources

. . . originates in the Vieux-Colombier

The Vieux-Colombier has become a legend.

Among those who know the history of this theatre, there are many who know nothing about its school.

This was situated at the side of the theatre, and had its home in a primitive hut which was scrubbed out every day with soap.

There are so many things to tell about it!

Figure 16 Etienne Decroux created *Duet in the Parc Saint-Cloud* on Steven Wasson and Corinne Soum, in 1983–4. Photograph by Paul McKenzie.

Figure 17 *Duet in the Parc Saint-Cloud.* Photograph by Paul McKenzie.

I would like to relate everything.

And above all:

The role of Suzanne Bing, our formidable leader.

Zealously rising to the demands of her task, she forgot herself in its execution.

And she is forgotten.

The running of a drama school worthy of the name presupposes the presence of an exceptional being, about whom it would be impossible to say: 'If she hadn't been there, someone else would have taken her place.'

Without her, the school would have remained nothing more than a project, or ended up like the others: chaos.

My own profound experience with schools, already spanning sixteen years, entitles me to say, without being accused of yielding to the pleasure of euphoria:

Without Suzanne Bing, there was no one.

Given this hypothesis, Copeau would have devoted himself to his theatre – a perpetual fire that one becomes obsessed with extinguishing – and the school would not have seen the light of day.

At any rate, not that day.

Thus everything which originated in this austere and marvellous hut would not have come forth into the world.

There, future actors were given the following classes: ground acrobatics, stadium athletics, ordinary gymnastics, classical ballet, corporeal mime, voice production, ordinary diction, declamation of classical chorus and of Japanese Noh, singing and sculpting.

History of music, of costume, of philosophy, of literature, of poetry, of theatre and of much more besides.

Other schools have a programme similar to this one.

But if, at about five o'clock, the street is crowded with parked cars, then today is the director's class.

The 'ladies' attend no other.

They do mime in tea-gowns and Louis XV heels.

How come?

How can they think that mime can be practised in such dress, and without any previous training in classical ballet, which, moreover, their school offers them?

Let me reply for them:

First of all, hoping to be noticed that day by the director, they accept mime as a part of society theatre, which is related to film, which is in turn a part of tasting the heady delights of diversity.

In the best of cases, they hope that the great man will infuse them with knowledge in the form of a cocktail.

For they want to climb upwards by letting themselves slide downwards.

That is why they only attend the course – I was going to say, court – of the director.

You can imagine how pernicious their presence is.

Everyone agrees on this, but . . . they do pay.

I cannot imagine Copeau putting up with these creatures. If someone had proved to him that the money of these ladies was indispensable to the life of his school, he would have closed it.

We were obliged to attend all the classes.

In fact, we never even dreamed that they could be voluntary.

Better yet, during my first year, Jacques Copeau did not teach a single lesson.

I think he was busy teaching the teachers.

What would have become of our 'ladies', who could only study the alphabet with the secretary of the Académie, only study exercises at the barre with Nijinsky, the piano with Paderewski and addition with Henri Poincaré?

As it turned out, famous people were not lacking but that did not lead to films. Mlle Lamballe from the Opéra, the Fratellinis, Jules Romains, Louis Latzarus the composer, and Marc the sculptor.

One moment the pupil's costume was that of the runner, the next that of the sculptor.

Be reassured! Amidst all this youthfulness there were minor dramas of love and flirtation; but work fell on these involvements as cool air on top of hot.

I have not forgotten that I did the most valuable work with artists who were not very famous at the time: Georges Vitray for diction, George Chennevière for general education, Garcia Mansilla for voice production, Jean Dorcy and Mlle Copeau for corporeal art in general.

The latter, known today by the name of Marie-Hélène Dasté, was a young girl whom we addressed as *tu*, and whom we called Maïène (a contraction of Marie-Hélène).

Joining in our pranks with a knowing smile, she was nevertheless the chain that bound us to discipline, but in the form of a flexible and blossoming liana.

In Copeau's authority there was theocracy, in Suzanne Bing's there was asceticism.

This could have made our lives morose.

Thanks to Maïène, who inherited three-quarters of her smile from her mother, this was not the case at all.

What a happy trinity!

Of the theatre and the school, we knew that Copeau preferred the latter.

Which could not help but give rise to a polite and unofficial rivalry between students and actors.

The director, more demanding than his public, judged his productions in terms of his goals, not in terms of popular success.

A theatre budget and the service of the Idea sometimes have divergent requirements.

The dénouement came in January 1924: he closed his theatre and took his school to Burgundy in order to set up his winter quarters there.

It seems to me that this decision was a revolt against the social mechanism: 'This theatre depends necessarily on the past: it is managed by its actors, who were trained in another school, and by its authors, who wrote plays without knowing beforehand to whom they would take them; since such management impedes development, we shall abandon the present but not the future.'

This is perhaps what he thought, for a characteristic of the director was an appetite for the absolute. In addition, he would not allow himself to be the submissive plaything of some vague determinism.

We had some good times in Burgundy and I think the failure could have been avoided.

But there came a time when, like germs that overcome us in moments of weakness, the difficulties of communal life won out.

These dissensions were always dignified.

Then came procreation by subdivision.

Copeau had ignited us so well that those who left him took the fire with them.

Each one, wishing to create his own Vieux-Colombier, had a chance to see how much effort is required, even in order to fail.

There was the *Compagnie des quinze* of Saint-Denis, the *Comédiens routiers* of Chancerel, the double-act Gille and Julien, my group *Une graine* and Dorcy's *Proscenium*.

These last two were on the level of amateur socialist propaganda.

Out of them rose this proliferation of mime and the speaking chorus in popular demonstrations.

As a film actor, Jean-Louis Barrault, equipped with the best talent, owes nothing to this movement.

But as a man of the theatre, he is the grandson of our school.

The Quatre Saisons, a theatre run by André Barsacq, was another grandson of our school. All this youthful theatre, the true avant-garde, the new cartel . . . originates in the Vieux-Colombier (school part).

When this art has achieved its maturity and its classicism, and when it therefore will have escaped the criticism caused by its present stage of experience – for it is a difficult art – it will be fitting to celebrate extravagantly the birthday of the founding of this school.

Each company will perform the best piece from its repertory; Gille and Julien will revive their number especially, and everyone will pay to the pioneers of the primitive hut the homage that they are owed.

CORPOREAL MIME
AT VIEUX-COLOMBIER
(SCHOOL)

We called it the mask.

Unlike Chinese masks, ours were expressionless.

Our bodies were as bare as decency would allow.

An indispensable measure. For, once the face was obliterated, the body needed all of its parts to replace it.

We mimed simple actions: a man pestered by a fly, wants to rid himself of it; a woman, disappointed by a fortune teller, strangles her; the actions used in trade or a sequence of movements made by a machine.

The manner of playing resembled the slow motion of film. But while that is the slowing down of fragments of reality, ours was the slow production of one gesture in which many others were synthesized.

This process, already intelligible, was beautiful.

We reproduced noises of the town, of the house, of nature, the cries of animals. All of this with the mouth, the hands and the feet.

In a rapid consultation – three minutes at the most – the pupils made up a sketch which they performed on the spot.

They alone knew what to expect or not to expect from this type of playing: they therefore had to be their own playwright. At the end of the '23–'24 season, they gave a performance before an invited audience.

Having completed only one year, I was not allowed to participate.

Sitting quietly among the spectators, I beheld an astonishing show.

It consisted of mime and sounds. The whole performance took place without a word, without any make-up, without costumes, without a single lighting effect, without properties, without furniture and without scenery.

The development of the action was skilful enough for them to condense several hours into a few seconds, and to contain several places in only one.

Simultaneously before our eyes we had the battlefield and civilian life, the sea and the city.

The characters moved from one to the other with total credibility.

The acting was moving and comprehensible, of both plastic and musical beauty.

We were in June 1924.

Productions which astonish people today, in no way surpass and do not always equal, what was done in that show.

(July, 1939)

GORDON CRAIG

Around 1900, sophisticated society's avant-garde still adheres to the doctrine of realism in art. In the theatre it is the reign of Stanislavsky and Antoine. Gordon Craig chooses this moment to launch his first fire-ships against realism. The tree he wants to burn is green.

In opposing realism, Craig is not showing himself to be an arch-conservative, for in his mind there is no question of maintaining the state of things attacked by Antoine. Since the style condemned by Antoine was ossified before it died, its abandonment was necessary. Antoine wanted to drive away this style without replacing it: 'Let us change forthwith the old conditions.'

'It was necessary.'

It was therefore against a realism consumed by its own offensive that Gordon Craig took up his own. Realism is troubled and looks askance at this meddler. Our hero thus constitutes the third force, wounding the two already opposed power-blocks, each of which seeks vengeance by pushing him towards the other.

It was on all theatrical fronts that Craig fought his battle: administration, direction, design, text, actor; the final goal was to change theatre into an original art. This does not mean an amazing theatre, for we already have several examples of that.

According to Craig, the stage, instead of being a brothel, since it is a meeting place for all the arts, first had to become the springboard of the movement. Concerning the actor, I have raised from memory the following seven points:

First point: when the actor performs, his mind must exploit his emotion and not his emotion his mind. The state of intoxication is to be particularly discouraged in a work of artifice.

Second point: style and symbol are qualities essential to art.

Third point: the actor must know his craft before appearing on stage. He should not play his hand in public, and his apprenticeship should last six years.

Craig does not say whether this apprenticeship consists of carrying on interminable discussions in cafes, that serve as casting agencies, or of 'doing scenes' in drama schools, that also serve as casting agencies; but he would have had to agree that we quickly become aware of the exemplary patience needed in the study of theatre.

Fourth point: the traditional actor exhibits explosions of his inner self and does so in front of everybody: this is immodest.

Fifth point: the actor must seek inspiration from the methods used by other artists.

Sixth point: the actor must also reject the advice of these other artists when they invade the stage in order to colonize it.

Seventh point: the laws of the theatre have yet to be found. What is urgent is their discovery, not just attempts based on guesswork.

APPARENT CONTRADICTIONS IN CRAIG

But it is here, in the most original point of his contribution, that Craig, like all prophets, seems to contradict himself.

I.

1. According to Craig, the actor is insufficient because his acting is realistic and more vocal than visual. Therefore his acting should have style and be more visual than vocal.

2. Craig then goes to great length to convince us that the body is incapable of obeying the mind's command, and therefore that we cannot count on it to manifest the poetry of drama.

3. Consequently, the actor must be replaced by an ideal marionette. So far, no contradiction.

II.

But then, at a later point, Craig informs us that his idea of replacing the actor with the marionette in question was merely a battle image and that he never seriously entertained such a prospect. So what is to be done? No traditional actor, no marionette, no corporeal actor: with what are we going to act?

III.

It is my opinion that we can get out of this categorical impasse by inferring that when Craig speaks of the impotence of the body, he is thinking only of the admittedly great, but surmountable difficulties experienced by the body when it attempts to obey the commands of the mind. And my reasoning is as follows:

1. If the marionette is, at least, the image of the ideal actor, we must consequently try to acquire the virtues of the ideal marionette.

2. We can only acquire these by practising a specially applied form of gymnastics, and this leads us to the mime known as corporeal.

IV.

Next, on one page of his well-known book, Craig has put a footnote: here the author declares himself in favour of mimed drama. This note, which I suppose was included as an afterthought, encourages me to think that I am headed in the right direction.

V.

Finally, Craig sees our show and writes an enthusiastic article about it [see pp. 24–7]. But he insists that his writings are not related to our performance.

Does he mean that between his writings and what we are doing, there is no causal relationship, such as father to son, or that he does not even see the relationship of brothers, or simply, a similarity of desire?

Now I am confused again.

And yet corporeal mime seems to answer Craig's claims so well.

1. *Discovering the law of the theatre?*

– Is there any method more scientific than that which undresses the actor in order to see what remains of him? A method that is based primarily and ultimately on depriving him of everything that is not part of his being: sets, costumes, properties, text? When the actor, left to himself, has discovered what he can and what he really cannot do, shall we not be able to see better what part was played by the things we have suppressed, and thus to what extent, and also to what end, we must reinstate what was dismissed?

2. *The mastery of emotion?*

– When the actor undertakes to express himself in lines of meticulous geometry, risking his balance and thus suffering literally in his flesh, he is indeed forced to hold back his emotion and behave as an artist – an artist of drawing.

3. *Modesty?*

– Only the face is immodest, since it alone reveals our inner self, that which we *are*. But the body has the ability to trace large lines through the air, which distract from the lines of our form. It thus replaces the design that we are, with the design that we want.

4. *Style and symbol?*

– It is enough, in a bare space that is devoid of words and devoid of music, to be naked oneself in order for style and symbol to become compulsory: they alone dress. The audience would never accept it if a man, stripped of his clothes, were to behave as a gentleman. The comedy would be indecent.

5. *The need for the visual aspect in the theatre?*

– *How can we dispense with it if we are offering nothing else?*

6. *Prolonged apprenticeship before performing?*

– What reveals our lack of preparation, when such is the case, is that it provokes a physical fall, thus protecting us from a moral one. The donkey believes himself a bishop too soon only because he is covered with the relics of a real priest. The actor, finding himself alone, quickly realizes what he is worth and dreads the end of his apprenticeship.

7. *Seeking inspiration from the method of the other arts?*

– We inquire about the technical aspect of the arts and achievements of a Rodin, a Maillol, an Ingres and a Signac; and also of a Boileau, a Banville and an Edgar Allan Poe, not just out of pure curiosity.

8. *Mistrusting other artists when they want to help the theatre without being naturalized?*

– Surely the time for this mistrust is past when we are alone on stage?

9. *Even if Gordon Craig wants to add to the actor a costume that has been better conceived; a scenic design; lighting; a set and a text that also have been better conceived; the actor whom we are to place in this better-conceived whole will still have to be better conceived himself. And I can see no other formula than to make the actor Robinson Crusoe.*

10. *As for the idea of replacing the actor with the super-marionette, I cannot help but imagine that, deep down, whatever he says, Craig must have considered this with due seriousness.*

I personally wish for the birth of this actor made of wood. I envision this large-scale marionette arousing, by its appearance and its movements, a feeling of seriousness and not of condescension. The marionette that we desire must not make us laugh or feel moved as does the playing of a young child. It must inspire terror and pity and, from there, rise to the level of the waking dream.

But it is necessary to construct such an instrument, and it is necessary to determine the nature of its movement. Is it not obvious that our way will have been substantially paved when the practice of Corporeal Mime becomes learned? After all, its movements already draw their breath from the cardinal lines of geometry.

But is it really important to know whether Craig declares himself for the marionette or for the human body; for the actor alone or as complemented by the other arts? Does it matter if he contradicts himself *or if I have misunderstood his thinking?* It does not matter that he writes sometimes as a pamphleteer, sometimes as a philosopher and sometimes as an artist; what counts is the idea suggested by the central current of his thought. The fact that the formula of his doctrine lends itself to a discussion on the nature of that doctrine *does not stop this last from being condensed.*

After having read Craig, rather than while reading him, we discern his path. Would the famous theatrical experiments of Russia in 1928 have ever seen the light of day if Craig's ideas had not spread across Europe at the beginning of the century?

– I wonder.

Contrary to what one might think, Craig is not a doctrinarian. Some of his reactions to the work of Stanislavsky have proved that his admiration encompasses an enormous area. Animated more by the spirit of delicacy than by the spirit of geometry, he appears to be a grand lord contemplating life; a man of the world standing apart from the world. He has written that my faith is ferocious. His is not. It is fine, sensitive and as imperishable as discretion.

Finally, Craig is not haughty or bitter or peevish. He rejoices at another's victory, as long as it is honestly won.

He is therefore one of the party and seems satisfied at having carried through his personal comedy successfully.

We have done well in choosing him as our leader.

Extract from a lecture given in Paris 6 November 1947 for the beginning of the new school year.

WHERE CRAIG ABSTAINS

(This text, which was to have been part of the November 6th, 1947 lecture on Gordon Craig, was not read because it would have made the lecture too long.)

Certain malicious minds have pointed out to us that Gordon Craig achieved nothing. I propose to prove that this refusal to act was as beautiful as a silence.

What honest statesman would agree to be government minister without first obtaining the means of executing the policy that glorifies his name?

– None. In like manner, if a dishonest man in similar conditions refuses any form of coronation, one can see no reason for his doing so other than madness.

Does he even have a policy?

– He has a pretext.

Does one reflect often enough that certain failures launch careers better and less dangerously than victories do?

I can think of certain directors who have hewn out of the ice one failure after another and then turned these steps into their stairway of honour.

On the subject of failures, there have been noble ones where the craftsman buried himself under the crumbling ruins of his creation. In agreeing to undertake it, such a man at least believed he possessed the means of finishing what he had to say.

Then he became rigid, launched the excessive quantity of his will and broke in two, to avoid having to bend.

There are thus two sorts of failure: that of the clear-sighted man and that of the visionary.

There have been noble victories, where the craftsman would not agree to being (what is called) elevated to (what is called) power before spending a lifetime in the catacombs of learning, where he could amuse himself while awaiting the Occasion. Such craftsmen also perished, but of old age, shortly after their victories, which were often dead before they were.

But the majority of those who think of themselves as supermen because they know they are above other men, are in reality kept afloat by them. Asked if they can find a difference between the realization of an idea and self-realization, they are, in fact, unable to do so.

Is taking one's life in order to be born, then again in order to survive, not a ridiculous idea?

A curious transaction among men: to sell your soul you must not have one.

In essence Baudelaire said that what interested him was not succeeding, but doing what he wanted to do.

Before saying that Craig was incapable of action, it is necessary to show us those who have done what Craig could not do, not what he did not want to do. There are men, I know, who attempted to embody Craig's doctrine: all were defeated while, as he foresaw, winning themselves a different victory on the side.

And of course we know their names and their astonishing performances, so ideal for charming those ladies who love to be frightened.

Craig, therefore, who was not incapable of foresight, is superior to these men.

The man who has seen straight and who sees straight every day either continues along his path or stays in one place. Patience is a long-term genius.

It is an offence to order a meal knowing in advance that one will not be able to pay for it. Craig is innocent of this.

When Lenin had passed age forty-six, and decided it was time to act, if this time had required endless waiting, and if Lenin had endlessly pursued his rich readings in Geneva, Aristide Briand, our very own renegade and pseudo-creator would have been the last person to give him lessons in socialist realism.

One must admit that this Briand was very likeable. As Balzac said: 'Men given to vice are always charming.'

There are days when the strength of soul consists of boiling then freezing in one's own silence. This could be seen under the Occupation, although the latter was only temporary. There is also the occupation of seats and how can we be scandalized by a world where all the seats belong exclusively to those who sit?

That is why one has difficulty in imagining a theatre on its feet.

The realization of a goal related to Craig's ideal was to come from Soviet Russia in 1927, because the means were available.

The general misery encouraged people to be actors.

The young and talented did not hurl themselves into the monster Cinema, which elsewhere steadfastly mows them down.

The coquetry of revolution: the Russian state was clever enough to want to provide the sustenance of preparation.

It was therefore entitled to impose upon its actors beneficial requirements which included gymnastics, classical ballet, acrobatics, etc.

When he said that the task could not be completed in the western state of things, Craig had therefore seen clearly.

Let the man who triumphs without the necessary weapons, where Craig would have liked to triumph, cast the first stone.

Let the man who saw clearly, throw him the first flower.

(*On the subject of 'achievement', the Gordon Craig Exhibition organized in Paris at the Bibliothèque Nationale in May, 1962 showed Craig's important career as actor, director and designer. – A. Veinstein)

Autobiography relative to the genesis of Corporeal Mime

My predispositions

In order to transform things, man touches them.

If he cannot do so with his hand, he touches them with a tool, which he is touching.

Of the Fine Arts, I prefer those that represent touch and being touched, which are practised by means of touch and whose finished product can be touched by an appreciator.

I should like to have been a sculptor.

The spirit becomes clear only when filtered through stone.

Statuary is an art carved out of reality and one whose creations are permanent. The model of the sculptor is the transformer that touches and is touched and whose name is man. In transforming stone, the sculptor touches it, and once his work is finished, we can touch it.

I should like to have been a poet.

I prefer rhythmical poetry, since it seems to me that, in order achieve rhythm, it is necessary to sculpt language.

It is my desire that the actor accept the artifice and sculpt the air, making us feel where the line of poetry begins and where it ends.

I was born to love mime.

The body is a glove whose finger is thought.

Pensée, poussée, pouce et pincée, which in French are almost homonyms, are also almost synonyms. ('Thought, pushed, thumb, pinched.') Our thought pushes our gestures in the same way that the thumb of the sculptor pushes forms; and our body, sculpted from the inside, stretches. Our thought, between its thumb and index-finger, pinches us along the reverse flap of our envelope and our body, sculpted from the inside, folds.

Mime is, at the same time, both sculptor and statue.

Thus its witness stands up to re-touch the world.

Another motive

I was gifted.

Imitating is easy for me and amuses me.

My muscles are strong and supple. I have rhythm.

I design in space as if I were seeing myself. I analyse easily and I explain easily.

I was thus created for doing and for demonstrating.

I say this out of modesty, since this is a selfish motive.

I say all this out of honesty, for, since doctrine is often a systemization of desires, I felt it was my duty to pass on this information.

Revelation in Three Phases

So if a serious motive for the decision to dedicate yourself to mime is that you have it in you, in the stomach of your mind, so to speak, this serious motive is not enough. You can only devote yourself to an image. An image exists before the eyes. You cannot admire yourself because you are behind your own eyes.

What, then, did I see that made me decide? Who was responsible for the idea taking shape within me, that corporeal mime could be an art of the Beautiful and thus merit the dedication of a lifetime?

– The café-concert, Georges Carpentier and Jacques Copeau.

At the Café-Concert des Bateaux parisiens, a wooden construction on a Seine embankment

I once saw an act there, entitled 'Attraction'.

Three policemen were pursuing three crooks. Shortly

afterwards, the crooks were pursuing the policemen, who nonetheless kept on chasing the crooks.

Here is one of the policemen, climbing up a ladder; but here a crook, catching him in the act, hurls at the policeman's back an enormous knife, which sticks into it, vibrating. Then a second, then a third.

Then the policeman, in order not to miss anything, stays anchored on his rung and, so that we should not miss anything, turns his face towards us, roaring as if to say:

'Heavens, how it tickles!'

And, his back shuddering with nervous voluptuousness, like a fish in distress, he shakes his banderilla from side to side.

So that the knife, moving in this way, becomes an external expression of the internal spasm.

And there were many other climactic moments . . . !

This was in 1909. I was eleven years old.

Although this act was just the skeleton of a story, with no moral and no depth of character, it was an example of corporeal mime.

The actors lived their story, unconscious of being heroes, and therefore did not express it.

They abstained from those facial gymnastics, which certain mimes use to try to communicate what they could do or say to us.

With great restraint their faces expressed the state of the hero in action, without distracting us from the bodies which were performing that action. And yet am I right in claiming that they were expressive? – They had a certain manner.

The action was embellished by dangerous juggling and acrobatics: nothing was gratuitous; it was all an integral part of the story.

About the same time, I saw a Pierrot who told his audience, without words, the tale of his love, his misfortune, his crime and his punishment.

The speaking actor is less garrulous.

This displeased me.

Georges Carpentier

Around 1908, in different places, there came into being an idea and a fact; later, for society at large, the idea will become a postulate and in fact a practice. (As far as this is possible.) Obesity is no longer a reference point; skill outdoes strength; the slender man makes his entrance.

Wrestling gives way to boxing.

Ovals confront squares.

Young men who look like students appear in the ring.

It is at this moment that a champion arrives on the scene. Although he comes from a family of miners, he is the archetype of the athletic student. He is fifteen years old.

It is Georges Carpentier.

Vigour and grace; strength, elegance; dazzle and thought; a taste for danger and a smile.

He never cheated. In the arena this miner's son became, or remained, a man of the world.

He was the protective eldest brother adored by the youngest.

And all of this because being slim, strong and handsome, he set out to punish bullies.

We would never suspect that he was the motivating image for our study of physical mime (tragedy section).

Jacques Copeau

The act to which I referred belonged to the performing arts, but was comic and superficial.

The boxer Carpentier was a noble model, but he was reality.

The idea of a performing art that represents through body movement, that could shelter under its vast roof not only that which causes laughter but also that which arouses terror, pity and the waking dream, still remained to be found. Now it had been found.

It had already been put into practice at the Vieux-Colombier school.

All I invented was my belief in it.

One of the exercises at this school consisted of performing short plays, many of which were tragic, with the face covered but the body almost naked.

DOCTRINAL MANIFESTO

This study of mime was regarded by Jacques Copeau as but a small part of the study of spoken theatre, and as having two aims: that the body should not contradict what the voice tells us; and that on those occasions when the actor acts in silence, the dramatic illusion should not be lost.

It did not take me long to decide that the causal relationship of the two arts in question ought to be reversed. Instead of seeing in our mime one of the preparations for the spoken theatre, I saw in the spoken theatre one of the preparations for our mime, for mime had, in practice, been revealed as the more difficult.

Mime, I thought, has better things to do than complete another art.

Since it can grow to be self-sufficient, superior to the theatre and equal to dance, from which it differs in its roots, it must build itself up.

If others consider it only as a means, it has the right to consider itself as an end. Even more so because mime is the essence of theatre, which in turn is the accident of mime.

Theatre is a mixture of arts at the heart of which is the actor prematurely enclosed in a frame.

Almost everything in it retains the smell of reality; almost nothing in it transports us to the realm of memory or imagination.

Having seen in a museum the creations of Egypt or of Impressionism, one returns home ashamed of being an actor.

And yet this theatre offers us a life rich in dramatic situations when our lives are poor in them; therefore the life that it displays is more entertaining than reality, but not at all transformed.

It enriches the spectator more often with gold than with light.

The only event shown here is the event itself.

Let the riches be those that we already touch, but let them be multiplied. That is what we ask of this theatre; it is probably what was asked of Jesus when he multiplied the loaves and the fishes. And this materialistic dream, valid at the level of everyday existence, is embodied by the theatre, which thinks that it is painting heaven by removing the spaces between the pearls of life.

(January, 1948)

2
Theatre and mime

My definition of theatre

to Georges Pomiès[9]

PARTIAL INCARNATION
OF THE FUTURE ACTOR

I

The large number of elements that generally go into the composition of the theatre must contain material for a definition. . . . So what do we find? Worthy arts, each gifted with the power to capture the Universe in its studio, and which should not wish for either expansion or branches. Yet in a place called theatre we find painter, sculptor, architect, musician, singer, dancer and actor united together in an effort to produce something grand. The 'closed to the public' sign which adorns the entrance door to the stage was therefore not put up for them. But let there be no mistake: every art that has access to the stage also has a rigid code allowing it to express in its particular way everything that exists. Under no circumstances does the painter need to cover his canvas with protuberances in order to give the impression of a mountain. Painting expects no help from the outside: a flat surface suffices and if, in certain difficult spots, it flirts with scenic volume, this is done merely to taste the forbidden fruit or to supplement the actor's imagination, never out of need. With this example before us, let us boldly underline the rule: every art enjoys the privilege of expressing the world in its own way, without calling on any other art.

This is why they all, with one exception, avoid using up their leisure-time in this house of ill-repute, for they have all built a country house. But where is the *pied-à-terre* for the art of the actor? Where is its consolation? And its right to solitude? Does it have only a stone on which to rest its head? Where does one see the art of the actor as one sees painting: in its pure state?

Nevertheless, this hobo of the arts will not spit on paintings for vengeance, nor will it converse with statues in order to create a synthetic art, nor will it drape itself over monuments to adorn them with its visible presence.

Nor will it go to recite Corneille at Colonne concerts or perform the role of a satyr in a *corps de ballet*. What then? As though it were the Cain of the Muses and condemned to a perpetual reminder of its insufficiency, all its brothers overwhelm it with their support, give it fraternal help in walking sideways and wipe its mouth at the table; but, though they seem to provide sustenance, none of them would let it in their house, even to scrub the floor.

After such lavish kindness, we end up with this jewel:

Musical accompaniment to the spoken recitation of a poem.

In the light of this particular collaboration we can reflect on the general collaboration of the actor with other art forms, and ask if his protectors did not stretch out their arms just to stifle him.

Meanwhile, we are approaching the port of the definition, so let us try to land: since the actor is the only artist without a home of his own, the theatre must become his property.

Such a measure will not force him to drive out his old colonizers, but will enable him, finally free, to make his open-houses less frequent.

II

Of all the people with claims to the stage, only one has never been absent from it: the actor.

Music, dance and song are but occasional visitors; architecture holds its own, but only in cardboard; and painting, squashed against the canvas in an alcoholic stupor, has never been very regular: Shakespeare preferred signposts to painting; certain directors have replaced it with architecture; and Japanese Noh produces not only every act but also every play in the same set, with the result that architects and painters, familiar with the hardships of unemployment, are reduced to working in their own profession.

That leaves literature. 'The lawful wife', they say.

In reality, the most clinging concubine. This dragon of virtue, this respectable sorceress, did, however, once rush off on an adventure: it was in the sixteenth century, in the period of the Commedia dell'arte, when the actor, happy bachelor, could cook for himself: good times.

Alas! Dame Literature, back at home 'just for a bit', as she put it, to sew on a trouser-button, made the most of it and went through all the laundry; a week later and her roots were wriggling in the foundation.

Even in productions with words there are silences during which the actor meditates and develops; long moments during which the text is of no value and in which the actor creates emotion through the way he acts. Does the converse exist?

Have we ever, for even a second, heard a text without the speaker? Never, of course.

The only art unceasingly present on the stage is therefore the art of the actor.

III

The arts united in the theatre obey only the actor's orders; that is obvious. They all help him to create the illusion of reality and also to sweeten the unsavouriness of his work.

The painter and the (scenic) architect locate the action – this is prudent: it is distracting to imagine oneself in a bargain basement when in Agamemnon's palace – music, song and dance give life to the action; and literature, supporting with both arms at once, strews the action with paper flowers with one hand, while explaining with the other.

The only proof I need that the art of the actor is anaemic is the speed with which one passes from the audience to the proscenium and then onto the stage; the actor is nevertheless the master of the house: doddering, admittedly, but still the boss.

To imagine that one day these guests will say to their host: 'It's up to you, who speak as if you were in charge, to leave,' or to imagine the day when people will employ actors like Châtelet extras, does not imply a sense of prophecy.

And when we see skilful technicians and lighting designers who would make God ashamed of his sunset, rushing in for the kill, this prediction is indeed coming true.

We try not to think that, as an intermediary phase, the actor will become the announcer in a revue about the latest discoveries of the property master.

But whatever happens, the actor will remain the harmonic centre of the other arts, the orchestral conductor with perhaps rather faulty aim, but the tuning-fork of the theatre and, even if he is replaced by delightful silk puppets, it will still be philosophical and correct to remark: 'He is respected, therefore he was.'

IV

What will our definition be? We have seen that the actor is the only artist without a home of his own.

This encourages us to put him up in the theatre. We have seen that every art occupying the stage is still governed by the action, which is nothing more than the actor in motion: this makes us inclined to see him as 'the rightful inhabitant of the venerable tower'. We have seen above all – and this is decisive – that the actor is the only artist eternally present in the theatre. Such a statement eliminates all the other arts.

Indeed, a definition contains no properties other than the essential, and the essential is without exception the vital property of a thing. Since all the arts except that of the actor have suspended their services, at least for an instant, none other is the essential of theatre.

Put another way: none can be included in its definition.

That leaves us to find the logical form of this definition, which we shall express in substance as follows:

Theatre is the actor art.[10]

IVa

So those who define theatre as a 'synthesis of all the arts' have their answer. But a misunderstanding will shock our uninformed partisans. By an incorrect interpretation of the term 'definition', they will think that exceeding it is forbidden: an error to be dispelled by an example: to define man as a thinking animal does not stop him from getting dressed; but to define man as a thinking animal that wears clothes would make him lose all hope of ever taking a bath.

If scenery, along with other accidents, is no more essential to theatre than a jacket is to man, this does not prevent the actor from appearing inside a set any more than it does a man from appearing in a detachable collar. The converse does not exist: if theatre were defined as a synthesis of all the arts or even two of them, any dramatic effort to suggest scenery, words, music, etc., would be driven from the stage.

Theatre is the actor art.

V

What does all this prove? . . . That if the actor art on its own produces pure theatre, then our theatre is suffocating under a heap of rubble. In theatre companies one expects success from a good writer, and disaster from a bad one. The evil is so deeply rooted that it is revealed in the vocabulary: what we call 'play' is the printed text.

Here is the remedy:

1. For a period of thirty years, the proscription of every alien art. We shall replace the drawing- room setting with the

setting of the theatre itself, our intention being solely to provide a background for all imaginable actions.

2. For the first ten years of this thirty-year period: proscription of any elevation on stage, such as stools, staircases, terraces, balconies, etc. The actor will have to give the impression that he is higher and his partner lower, when in reality they are side by side.

Later, the authorization of certain forms of elevation on the condition that they create even greater challenges for the actor.

3. For the first twenty years of this thirty-year period: the proscription of any vocal sound.

Later, the acceptance of inarticulate cries for five years.

Finally, words accepted for the last five years of the thirty-year period, but invented by the actor.

4. After this period of war: stability. Plays shall be composed in the following order:

A. Rough outline of the written action serving as a basis for work.

B. The actor miming his action, then accompanying it with inarticulate sounds, then improvising his text.

C. Introduction of a dramaturge to translate the text into choice language, without adding a word.

D. Reappearance of alien arts, but practised by the actors. And when the actor is master in his own home he shall see to the employment of dancers, singers and musicians for indispensable and well-defined tasks. And then we shall see on the poster: text arranged by Mr Secondo.

But is this really the remedy?

There is no proof that, by its progress, pure theatre will compensate for the loss of the auxiliary arts, just as there was no proof that drawing would reproduce distance, and painting would reproduce light. The undertaking does not furnish the proof. What is worse, it requires will-power and imagination. It is a matter of cutting off the theatre's right hand.

(*1931.*)

This article, born thirty years ago, was my first proper piece of writing on art. And it was published!

In a review for fellow actors, roneotyped on grey, easily crumpled paper.

Its readers, young theatre people, used to spend all night talking in the street. It is for them that the article speaks: sitting, standing, stepping out. I must have written it while putting on my make-up.

Let us leave it with its needlessly risky formulas, on the edge of the question. When my past returns to me, I have no desire to amend it. I still believe in the main points, namely: that one must rehearse a play before writing it; and that the theatre is the actor art, which proves that, as an art of the beautiful, theatre does not exist.

(New York, March 10, 1962.)

Before being complete, art must be

The first time that I appeared as a professional actor was with Gaston Baty in about 1925.

Today my former employer, granting me a discussion with him, seems unaware that I was his apprentice.

In order to express myself with clarity, I have adopted an affirmative style . . . always pedantic and tinged with insolence.

But may Monsieur Gaston Baty not forget that I am happy to remain not only his cordial but also thoroughly respectful servant, and that I find it easy to express the gratitude which is his due.

In the open letter that he was kind enough to write to me, I note, apart from his delightful praise, the following reservations:

'Theatre is the only complete art, capable of totally expressing the soul and the world.'

'The others come into being when one of theatre's methods of expression lives by itself and declares itself independent; they are like the silver change from a gold coin. When Decroux tries to isolate from the dramatic process the mimic element, which he likes for its own sake, he is once more mutilating the major art for the benefit of a manifestation which is, in spite of everything, minor.'

'Such an amputation does not even offer us a body from which a limb has been severed, but instead the limb from which the body has been severed.'

'And the danger is all the greater because Decroux's talent is great.'

Here is my reply.

I think that an art is all the richer for being poor in means.

Music-hall has the maximum of means, and is poor.

Statuary has the minimum of means, and is rich.

I think that an art is complete only if it is partial.

The viewer's impression is artistic only if he makes comparisons.

I once heard a Parisian street urchin, admiring a real flower, exclaim:

– 'Oh, how beautiful! It looks just like a fake.'

You hear people commenting on an artificial flower:

– 'Oh, how beautiful! It looks just like a real one.'

With happy prospects, people speak of *la vie en rose*.

Why do people prefer saying that to *la vie heureuse* (the happy life)?

People also say:

A pale voice, the roundness of a sound, the colours of a text, the tone of a newspaper, the weight of a thought, the warmth of a heart.

On the subject of dance, one uses words of incantation, of cantilena.

Comparison = emotion.

The comparison in question occurs without our knowledge.

If the viewer's essential emotion is caused by comparison, the latter must be made possible.

It becomes so only if a partial art gives the idea of one world by means of another world: if it gives, for example, the idea of colour by presenting a colourless shape, or the idea of the shape by presenting a shapeless colour.

To give the idea of movement by attitude, of attitude by movement, of concrete by abstract and of abstract by concrete:

That is what is interesting.

As soon as you hit one part of a gong, the whole gong resounds, whatever part is hit.

Before being one thing or another, a thing must be.

Before being complete, an art must exist.

Our mime, which tries to suggest the life of the mind by using only the movement of the body, will be, if it succeeds, a complete art.

It would not take much for theatre not to be an art, since it suggests the thing by the thing itself: fatness by a fat man, woman by a woman, the body by a body, the word by the word, elevation by elevation, displacement by displacement, coloured volume by coloured volume.

The sideshow exhibiting the bearded woman, the giant and the dwarf, the hydrocephalic child and the two bodies linked by a single head, is a foreshadowing of orthodox theatre or of its perfected form: the cinema.

There an actor's weakness becomes a spectacle that hides the truth.

And among these weaknesses must be counted the charm of an actress and the good looks of an actor, which cloud our judgement by erecting a noiseless barrier between the acting and the audience.

If the theatre affects us, it does so as a crime affects us, seen through a window: Life already contains dramatic moments of its own: the loved one's suffering, his cure; the evil man's victory, his punishment.

Is the emotion that the sight of such misery and such relief causes us sufficiently impartial?

After all, what fever there is in the theatre.

Whereas a museum keeps alive in our soul all the purity of morning.

So if anyone retaliates by saying that, even without my beloved comparisons, orthodox theatre engenders emotion, we can reply:

– Yes. And the strongest of all.

But it is not that of the fine arts. When one savours a work of art, *C'est avec le palais et non avec le ventre* (it is with the palate and not the belly), as the poet Miguel Zamacoïs says of wine.

Orthodox theatre, scarcely being an art, has little chance of being complete.

It has been said that of all the arts, theatre is the most popular because it is the most direct.

I do not think that is a compliment.

For comparison is not 'direct'.

To compare is not to go from one point to another by the shortest route.

It is to dally, to leave the main road and wander part of the way down the lanes that cross it. Comparison is a luxury.

People of leisure, if they are cultured, have need of art.

People who are poor in everything above all long for stories.

To sum up: for art to be, the idea of one thing must be given by another thing. Hence this paradox: an art is complete only if it is partial.

For those who, as I do, like quotations, here are two:

> *Les parfums, les couleurs et les sons se répondent.*
> (Perfumes, colours and sounds correspond.)
>
> Charles BAUDELAIRE

> *Le monde est en entier présent dans chaque objet.*
> (The whole world is present in every object.)
>
> Georges CHENNEVIÈRE
> (*1942.*)

This article, with its air of clarity and its appearance of suffocating the subject under examination, troubles me.

Perhaps it is trying to prove an idea which exists only in the subconscious.

It is, admittedly, an attractive idea to represent the Cosmos besieged by the arts, each of which attacks a gate reserved for it alone, and which seeks the heart as a target for its battering ram.

But this subject deserves as much reflection as one is bold enough to allow oneself.

I therefore uphold this article precisely because of its inconclusiveness.

(New York, 10 March 1962.)

Figure 18 *They are Looking at Something Else,* created by Etienne Decroux for Denise Boulanger and Jean Asslin c. 1977. Photograph by Pierre Desjardins.

Figure 19
*They are
Looking at
Something
Else.*
Photograph
by Pierre
Desjardins

9   French modern dancer and cinema actor, Pomiès (1902-33)
     created innovative work sponsored by Charles Dullin and
     Gaston Baty. See the book about his life and work, *Danser c'est
     vivre*, Editions Pierre Tisné, Paris 1939.

10   Translator's note: Decroux's *original l'art d'acteur* is as
     awkward in French as 'the actor art' is in English.

Bibliography

Artaud, Antonin (1988) *Selected Writings*, trans. Helen Weaver, ed. Susan Sontag, Los Angeles: University of California Press.

Barrault, Jean-Louis (1972) *Souvenirs pour demain*, Paris: Editions du Seuil.

—— (1984) *Saisir le présent*, Paris: Editions Robert Laffont.

Bellugue, Paul (1963) *A propos d'art de forme et de mouvement*, Paris: Librairie Maloine.

Benhaim, Guy (1992) 'Le Mime Corporel selon Etienne Decroux', dissertation, University of Nice Sophia Antipolis.

Cadilhac, Paul-Emile (1931) 'L'Heure du ballet', *L'Illustration* 4616, 22 August, 563–8. [Article includes two photographs and one drawing of the Cambodians, misidentified as the 'ballet royal du Cambodge'.]

Chamberlain, Franc and Ralph Yarrow (eds) (2002) *Jacques Lecoq and the British Theatre*, London: Routledge/Harwood.

Craig, Edward Gordon (2009) *On the Art of the Theatre*, London: Heinemann.

Decroux, Etienne (1985) *Words on Mime*, trans. Mark Piper, ed. Thomas Leabhart, Claremont (CA): *Mime Journal*.

Fulchignoni, Enrico (1990) 'Oriental Influences on the Commedia dell'Arte,' trans. Una Crowley, *Asian Theatre Journal* 7 (1), 29–41.

Gordon, Mel (1974) 'Meyerhold's Biomechanics', *The Drama Review* 18 (3), 73–88.

—— (1984) 'Reconstructing the Russians', *The Drama Review* 28 (3), 11–16.

Hideo, Sasagawa (2005) 'Post/colonial Discourses on the Cambodian Court Dance', *Southeast Asian Studies* 42 (4), 418–41.

Lecoq, Jacques (1987) *Le Théâtre du geste*, Paris: Bordas.

Lehmann, Hans-Thies (2006) *Postdramatic Theatre*, trans. Karen Jürs-Munby, New York: Routledge.

Lorelle, Yves (1974) *L'Expression corporelle du mime sacré au mime du théâtre,* Paris: La Renaissance du Livre.

Murray, Simon and John Keefe (2007) *Physical Theatres: A Critical Introduction*, Abingdon: Routledge.

Nagy, Peter and Philippe Rouyer (eds) (1994) *The World Encyclopedia of Contemporary Theatre*, vol. 1: *Europe*, London: Routledge.

Pitches, Jonathan (2006) *Science and the Stanislavsky Tradition of Acting*, London: Routledge.

Ponder, Harriet W. (1936) *Cambodian Glory*, London: Thornton Butterworth.

Preston, Carrie J. (2005) 'The Motor in the Soul: Isadora Duncan and Modernist Performance', *Modernism/Modernity* 12 (2), 273–89.

Pronko, Leonard (1967) *Theatre East and West*, Los Angeles: University of California Press.

Rudlin, John and Norman H. Paul (eds) (1990) *Copeau: Texts on Theatre*, London: Routledge.

Savarese, Nicola (2001) '1931: Antonin Artaud Sees Balinese Theatre at the Paris Colonial Exposition', trans. Richard Fowler, *The Drama Review* 45 (3) (Autumn), 51–77.

Welby-Everard, Miranda (2006) 'Imaging the Actor: The Theatre of Claude Cahun', *Oxford Art Journal* 29 (1), 1–24.

Wylie-Marques, Kathryn (1998) 'Zeami Motokiyo and Etienne Decroux: Twin Reformers of the Art of Mime', in *Zeami and the No Theatre in the World*, ed. Benito Ortolani and Samuel L. Leiter, New York: Center for Advanced Studies in Theatre Arts.

Index

Related titles from Routledge

Etienne Decroux
(Routledge Performance Practitioners)

by Thomas Leabhart

Etienne Decroux is known as the father of modern mime. His practice and theory of corporeal mime are credited with elevating mime to the level of artistic autonomy that it enjoys today.
This is the first book to combine:

- An overview of Decroux's life and work
- An analysis of Decroux's 'Words on Mime', the first book to be written about this art
- A series of practical exercises offering an introduction to corporeal mime technique.

As a first step towards critical understanding, and as an initial exploration before going on to further, primary research, *Routledge Performance Practitioners* are unbeatable value for today's student.

Hb: 978–0–415–35436–3
Pb: 978–0–415–35437–0

Available at all good bookshops
For ordering and further information please visit:
www.routledge.com

Related titles from Routledge

Jacques Lecoq
Routledge Performance Practitioners series

Simon Murray

All books in the *Routledge Performance Practitioners* series are carefully designed to enable the reader to understand the work of a key practitioner. They provide the first step towards critical understanding and a springboard for further study for students on twentieth century, contemporary theatre and theatre history courses.

This text offers a concise guide to the teaching and philosophy of one of the most significant figures in twentieth century actor training. Lecoq's influence on the theatre of the latter half of the twentieth century cannot be overestimated.

This is the first book to combine

- an historical introduction to his life and the context in which he worked
- an analysis of his teaching methods and principles of body work, movement, creativity, and contemporary theatre
- detailed studies of the work of Théâtre de Complicité and Mummenschanz
- practical exercises demonstrating Lecoq's distinctive approach to actor training.

Hb: 978–0–415–25881–4
Pb: 978–0–415–25882–1

Available at all good bookshops
For ordering and further information please visit:
www.routledge.com

Related titles from Routledge

Theatre of Movement and Gesture

Jacques Lecoq

Jacques Lecoq was probably the most influential theorist and teacher of what is now known as physical theatre. *Theatre of Movement and Gesture*, published in France in 1987, is the book in which Lecoq first set out his philosophy of human movement, and the way it takes expressive form in a wide range of different performance traditions. Lecoq traces the history of pantomime, sets out his definition of the components of the art of mime, and discusses the explosion of physical theatre in the second half of the twentieth century.

This unique volume also contains:

- interviews with major theatre practitioners Ariane Mnouchkine and Jean-Louis Barrault;
- chapters by Jean Perret on Etienne Decroux and Marcel Marceau;
- a final section by Alain Gautre celebrating the many physical theatre practitioners working in the 1980s;
- a wealth of illustrations, including previously unpublished photographs from the Lecoq collection.

Lecoq's poetic, incisive writings form the backbone of this extraordinary text. The pieces gathered here represent a precious testimony to his special vision of the art of acting and of its close relationship with the history of mime and of masked performance.

Hb: 978–0–415–35943–6
Pb: 978–0–415–35944–3

Available at all good bookshops
For ordering and further information please visit:
www.routledge.com